MERCHANT IVORY'S

ENGLISH LANDSCAPE

MERCHANT IVORY'S

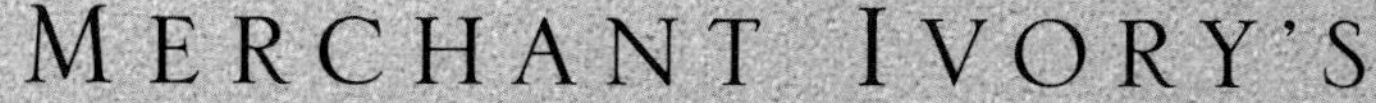

ENGLISH LANDSCAPE

ROOMS, VIEWS, AND ANGLO-SAXON ATTITUDES

JOHN PYM

WITH A FOREWORD BY JAMES IVORY

Harry N. Abrams, Inc., Publishers

TO H. A. P.

Project Manager: Margaret Rennolds Chace
Editor: Robbie Capp
Designer: Dana Sloan

LIBRARY OF CONGRESS CATALOGING-IN-PUBLICATION DATA

Pym, John.
Merchant Ivory's English landscape: rooms, views, and Anglo-Saxon attitudes/ John Pym; with a foreword by James Ivory.
p. cm.
Filmography: p
Includes index.
ISBN 0–8109–4275–5
1. Merchant Ivory Productions. 2. Motion picture locations—England—Guidebooks. 3. England—Guidebooks. I. Title.
PN 1999.M38P89 1995
791.43'025'41—dc20 94–32106

Published in 1995 by Harry N. Abrams, Incorporated, New York
A Times Mirror Company

Printed and bound in Hong Kong

PAGE 1: Wilbury Park.

PAGES 2–3: Maurice: Mr. Ducie (Simon Callow) and his schoolboys on the dunes at Rye, Sussex.

Contents

Acknowledgments

For their help in the preparation of this book—and for their friendship during the last sixteen years in England, India, and the United States—I thank James Ivory, Ruth Prawer Jhabvala, and Ismail Merchant. I am grateful to James Ivory and Ruth Jhabvala, in particular, for allowing me to read the scripts of *A Lovely World* and *Three Continents*. I also wish to thank Paul Bradley, C. S. H. Jhabvala, Catherine Freeman, Richard Macrory, Christian McWilliams, and Kazuo Ishiguro for telling me much that I did not know. I am indebted to Mrs. Jhabvala's Neil Gunn Lecture for details of Ruth Prawer's family background (*Blackwood's Magazine*, July 1979); and to the Automobile Association's guide *Places to Visit in Britain* (1988) for information relating to the houses of England. Finally, I thank my daughter, Celia Pym, for checking the gazetteer. Responsibility for all the text, however, remains mine.

Note on the Text

Care has been taken to verify the gazetteer summaries at the end of each chapter. Readers planning excursions are advised, however, to confirm by telephone details of the opening times of houses, gardens, churches, museums, monuments, and scenic spots. Some houses used as locations in Merchant Ivory's four principal English films are not open to the public, and one, Badminton House, is open only by special arrangement.

MERCHANT IVORY'S ENGLISH LOCATIONS
CAMERA SYMBOLS INDICATE CHIEF SITES USED IN THE SHOOTING OF THE FOUR FILMS
"A ROOM WITH A VIEW" "MAURICE" "HOWARDS END" "THE REMAINS OF THE DAY"
CHESHIRE
DERBY
NOTTINGHAM
LINCOLN
STAFFORD
SHROPSHIRE
LEICESTER
NORFOLK
WEST MIDLANDS
CAMBRIDGE
SUFFOLK
WALES
NORTHAMPTON
WARWICK
HEREFORD & WORCESTER
BEDFORD
GLOUCESTER
OXFORD
BUCKINGHAM
HERTFORD
ESSEX
AVON
BERKSHIRE
WILTSHIRE
SURREY
KENT
HAMPSHIRE
SOMERSET
WEST SUSSEX
EAST SUSSEX
DEVON
DORSET
CORNWALL
ENGLISH CHANNEL
BRIDGNORTH
LUDLOW
UPPER ARLEY
BIRMINGHAM
COVENTRY
BRAMPTON BRYAN
BEWDLEY
KIDDERMINSTER
WORCESTER
HEREFORD
STRATFORD-UPON-AVON
ELY
CAMBRIDGE
RIVER CAM
RIVER SEVERN
GLOUCESTER
WOODSTOCK
OXFORD
BADMINTON
CHIPPING SODBURY
CHIPPENHAM
CORSHAM COURT
BRISTOL
BATH
LIMPLEY STOKE
NORTON ST. PHILIP
WESTON-SUPER-MARE
PRIDDY
FROME
GLASTONBURY
LONGLEAT
STONEHENGE
AMESBURY
NEWTON TONEY
WILTON
SALISBURY
YEOVIL
SOUTHAMPTON
ABINGDON
DORCHESTER
PEPPARD COMMON
HENLEY-ON-THAMES
WINDSOR
EGHAM
LONDON
RIVER THAMES
RIVER MEDWAY
BRASTED
WESTERHAM
SEVEN OAKS
PENSHURST
EDENBRIDGE
CHIDDINGSTONE
CRANBROOK
RYE
BRIGHTON
EXETER
POWDERHAM CASTLE
PLYMOUTH
DARTMOUTH
BLACKPOOL SANDS
N
S
E
W

The Remains of the Day: Miss Kenton (Emma Thompson) has called aside Mr. Stevens (Anthony Hopkins) to break the news that his father has just died.

Foreword

JOHN PYM WRITES in the text of this book about the two contrasting Englands that have lately appeared in Merchant Ivory's films—one peopled by heroes and angels, the other by devils. Writers like E. M. Forster and Jean Rhys were very much aware of these contrasting Englands, one bright, the other dark, and their books and thus our films are fired as much by skepticism and indignation as by affection and admiration—in the case of Jean Rhys, it is mostly the former. Henry James shows us the darker side of the English character, too, but so far, we have not taken up any of his "international" novels, staying with him on the American side of the Atlantic.

When I was a child growing up in Oregon, my father built me an elaborate castle (which I still have), with battlements, a keep, and a great hall. This was set into the open end of an alcove in my bedroom, and I positioned myself behind it, placing cannons on the ramparts and guards at the door. No one—especially my sister and her friends—dared come very near, nor did they much want to, seeing me scowling at them from across the towers. Inside my castle, life was as French as I could make it, with a Versailles-like ritual taken out of books I had read on the *ancien régime*. My father also made me a small guillotine, but with a wooden blade, which I much enjoyed playing with, and which I also still have. And in all the years that I amused myself with these things, I never thought of the English for a moment, except perhaps to envy their king for his extravagant coach, which I had seen in newsreels.

When finally I did start to think about the English a bit, it was because of their buildings, first glimpsed in newsreels—again—as a backdrop to the coronation of George VI, or in photographs of that event in the Sunday color supplements of the *Oregonian* and the *San Francisco Chronicle*. What I saw was London at its most imperial: Buckingham Palace, long and looming, like a featureless gray cliff; the Houses of Parliament and the tower of Big Ben forming a more interesting profile; Westminster Abbey, seemingly huge, but in fact rather small and cozy, with its rows of ermine-trimmed peers and peeresses, placing their coronets on their heads at the same grand moment; Admiralty Arch, embracing its throng of cheering people, as the procession of state coaches passed through. It was impossible not to be stirred by such places and such sights. I began to look more carefully at the background of the movies I was seeing which had an English story, movies like *The Four Feathers, That Hamilton Woman, Rebecca*. And did my ear not also pick up at these same movies, however unconsciously, the self-assured English accents, some wry or suavely mocking, some insolent, some smugly hypocritical, that came later to typify for most audiences watching *Howards End* or *The Remains of the Day* the way people are supposed to speak in Merchant Ivory films?

In the United States there was a famous series of miniature rooms created by a rich American woman named Narcissa Thorne. Scaled at one inch to the foot, these were perfect in every detail and were in essence a sort of minuscule history of interior design in France, England, and America. First exhibited at the 1939 world fairs in New York and San Francisco, they were finally put on permanent display at the Art Institute of Chicago, where I saw them again and again on trips to that city. The French rooms were my favorites, but I began to look at the English ones more carefully on return visits, and to compare them with their American equivalents. To my eye then, as now, they seemed cooler, more worldly, grander in their proportions and more sophisticated in their decoration than the American ones, which, however, had their interest, too. I knew these did not come up to the English rooms, but in their more modest way I found them as attractive and, moreover, felt instinctively that their history was also a part of my history: I could see that the early New England colonists lived in such and such a way, the Southern planters in another. All this had some reference to me. But, as I looked through the glass separating me from the tiny glittering shadow boxes of state-rooms in English country houses, there was no such connection, or would not be until *The Remains of the Day*, and the glimpse I got through little swagged windows of a perfect painted English landscape, hazy and unreal as a studio backdrop, did not intrigue me in the slightest.

So what happened to cause the British to transcend their toylike scale, and to turn them for me into living heroes and angels—or devils? It was getting to know them in India, I think, a place famed for bringing out the best in them—and sometimes the worst. The English friends I made there in the early 1960s were cast in the heroic mode, though they were threadbare heroes I have to say—people like the Kendals of the Shakespeariana troupe, whose adventures are described in *Shakespeare Wallah*. The Kendals were also my introduction to the world of the English stage in all its crotchety splendor. Geoffrey Kendal—a wandering Player King, irascible and mercurial—was the strolling embodiment, with his wife, Laura, and daughters, Jennifer and Felicity, of this great tradition. They carried the English stage to the far corners of the Empire. I was too wet behind the ears to connect them to any sort of tradition, or to see how that might serve me in the future. The Kendals were not quite as English by then as they had once been; they had lived in India for many years, and by the time of *Shakespeare Wallah*, they were there on sufferance, which is the story of the film. They felt at home in India, felt the country really *was* their home. They were not like the unspeakably disagreeable English people depicted in *Heat and Dust* and *A Passage to India*, who never gave an inch to the place or its people.

When, as an American, I think of the English now, I think of them as our closest cousins, as family members. I have also come to see how very, very tough they are, how strong. Americans hate physical discomfort and inconvenience, and we wallow too much in our feelings. The English stride about as if they personally do not have to bother with feelings very much. It may seem like heresy to admire such a quality at the end of the twentieth century, after decades and decades of being told and reading about how feelings count. Of course, there are celebrated cases that get into the British newspapers describing Her Majesty's government officials who stick too much to the letter of the

DIANA THE HUNTRESS GLANCES OVER HER SHOULDER AT A HALF-OPEN DOOR THROUGH WHICH, PERHAPS, AN ENGLISH MILORD IS ABOUT TO ENTER. A MINIATURE EIGHTEENTH-CENTURY ENGLISH DINING ROOM, FROM THE WORKSHOP OF MRS. JAMES WARD THORNE, AT THE ART INSTITUTE OF CHICAGO.

James Ivory listens to a sound playback on the beach at Rye, Sussex, during the shooting of *Maurice*. The fur-trimmed goggles, on loan from the prop department, are the sort of thing, Ivory said, that the English explorer Captain Scott might have taken with him to the Antarctic. "These goggles were Clive Durham's motoring goggles, but they kept the sand out of my eyes—until the ancient elastic band broke."

law, so that they are shown up as being shockingly indifferent to the suffering of helpless people, all because of some ludicrous-sounding and antiquated regulation. A grotesque case of this kind was reported in the English papers on April 29, 1994. A woman prisoner named Sue Edwards was kept handcuffed while she delivered her baby in a hospital. This grim episode, almost out of the eighteenth century, created a stir, but the Home Secretary rejected calls by the Labour Opposition for an enquiry, saying, as reported in the *Guardian*, "There appears to have been a misunderstanding over the guidelines." But personally speaking, I have almost always found a great deal of kindness and concern for others in England, and great good manners on the part of these favorite cousins.

Going back to emotions and feelings, it seems to me the English have somewhat unfairly earned the reputation through most of the world of being coldly distant, overly repressed with strangers who make friendly overtures, and secretive. I have often found them to be just as loquacious as Americans and as ready to tell a stranger the most intimate things about their lives, whether sitting on a train, in a pub, or side by side in an airplane. It's *I* who have ended up feeling too withdrawn or standoffish. And my goodness, how the witty things they say can make me laugh!

A word about nostalgia. Our English films are criticized by the British newspapers for being too nostalgic. They write that Merchant Ivory has done this deliberately, for commercial gain. They even call *The Remains of the Day* a piece of nostalgia. But nostalgic for whom? Are the tasks of swabbing parquet floors and polishing brass in the Old Manor so very wonderful to recall? The papers accuse us of presenting a sun-dappled world of large, attractive houses with many servants, where high tea is set out on spacious lawns before well-dressed "toffs," who live by a comforting social ritual that mirrors the certainties of the day (mostly pre-1914) in matters of personal morals and politics. But what business has it ever been of mine to transport the British public back to happier days, when the sun never set on the flag and all life's graces flowed reassuringly down from the monarch on his throne, through the middle classes to the man in the street, and even to the criminal in his—or her—cell? Americans do not much care about the Edwardian Age, can scarcely say when it happened, uninterested as we are in keeping the many English kings and queens straight. Americans, I think, are interested in what E. M. Forster and Kazuo Ishiguro (both with a bit of help from Ruth Jhabvala) had to say about some favorite cousins and all the elaborate workings of their minds and hearts. They hope to have the bright glass on the shadow box lifted, in order to peer more easily into its recesses.

—James Ivory

Emma Thompson, Anthony Hopkins, and James Ivory on the Grand Pier at Weston-super-Mare during the filming of *The Remains of the Day.*

Pages 14–15: Wilbury Park in an early morning mist. "The kind of scene," Ivory said, "that a cameraman can rarely capture, because by the time the crew has set up its tons of equipment, and shooting schedules being what they are, the mist has evaporated. So it was on this day."

Introduction

When I first met him, in 1978, Ismail Merchant had been producing feature films on three continents for sixteen years. He materialized one summer afternoon in the periodicals annexe of the British Film Institute, off Dean Street, Soho, in the West End of London. He was wearing a shining grey suit, gleaming black shoes, and a generous blue silk tie: his exuberance was uncontainable. He had come to see Penelope Houston, a friend since 1965, the year of his second film, *Shakespeare Wallah*, which she and her magazine, *Sight and Sound*, had been among the first to champion. He unfolded a trade paper and put down a white cardboard box tied with confectioners' ribbon. Inside was an almond cake topped with slices of glazed apple. He had, I believe, just signed an agreement with the National Film Finance Corporation, giving effect to his latest venture, *The Europeans.*

Our quarters were quiet and isolated; the telephone occasionally rang; reviews were composed on manual typewriters; articles arrived twice a day from faraway contributors to be processed with old-fashioned thoroughness. There was a dusty, semisweet aroma of Grip-Fix paste and Dunhill cigarettes. Weather permitting, we sat on the flat roof outside Penelope's cubbyhole and contemplated the balcony gardens, neglected brickwork, and higgledy-piggledy ventilation shafts of our Italian neighbours. We were left alone, and spared most of the routines of a public institution. We once attempted to grow tomatoes, and in the racing season, a television was turned on, from time to time, for Penelope to confirm, leaning against a doorpost with her back to the rest of us, the performance of a favoured horse.

"I have come to wake you up!" Ismail announced at the top of his voice, and only half joking. "But see how much I think of you," he added consolingly. "I have brought you the best cake in London. Sit down. Fetch a knife. . . . We are about to begin our best film, Penelope, from a novel by your favourite author, Henry James." Perhaps, I said, since I was shortly to be in Massachusetts, I could visit one of the New Hampshire locations, the house of Mr. Wentworth so shaken by the arrival of Baroness Münster, and talk to the scriptwriter, Ruth Prawer Jhabvala, if she was to be there. It might make a line or two for the magazine. The sun shone more brightly. "But of course!" Ismail said. "You will stay with us, I shall arrange it." And that was that. "Now, come, everyone, have another slice of this delicious cake." The command was emphasized by a gesture of impatience and generosity, as if to say, "How could you not accept another slice?"—now, this very second.

⁂

ISMAIL MERCHANT was born in Bombay shortly before the eruption of World War II. In April 1944, the explosion of a British ammunition ship devastated the Victoria and Princes docks in Bombay harbour, wrecking sixteen other ships and most of the dockside buildings and heavy equipment. Fire spread over one hundred acres. Ismail's home trembled and bricks fell through the roof. "We thought the Japanese had come," Merchant said. "We were convinced it was the end." Later, however, after the war, the expulsion of the British from India became the pressing issue. Ismail and his schoolfellows rode in open trucks, shook their fists, and paraded banners with such slogans as GO HOME, *FIRRUNGI!* (Go home, foreigner!)—the future producer's first determined attempt to rouse the English to positive action.

"Then there were the Hindu-Muslim riots," Merchant said. "I still have nightmares about them. Armed police would come to clear the streets. During the curfew we'd sit at home, sometimes for forty-eight hours, glued to the radio. Since newspapers were restricted, the BBC world news was very important to us, similarly a BBC programme of 'Readings from Great Writers.' The cook sneaked out to the bazaar to bring what he could find. (Food wouldn't keep so we had to eat whatever he bought immediately.) No one wanted the British to stay. But then, mixed up with that, was the idea of Partition, of 'India' and 'Pakistan.' Rioting was everywhere, black flags flew from buildings. It was a time of extraordinary turmoil."

Nationalist ferment and religious strife were not, however, the dominant themes of Ismail's childhood. His father, a devout Muslim, was a merchant with a broad and tolerant view of the world. He traded in both homespun cloth and high-quality English textiles, and was no less a patriot for his conviction that the public should have the opportunity to buy the best material, no matter where it came from. "I was told that to be a man of special ability, one must go to a place that teaches one to become an able person." Oxford and Cambridge, the venerated English universities, were, Ismail's father believed, and his son agreed, the ultimate destination for a professional person. "My parents wanted me to become a doctor or a lawyer. I wanted to know about law, but not about medicine. I disliked the idea of cutting up bodies. I thought the law would be useful, but I was not fascinated by it. What always attracted me was films."

It was accepted fact in the Merchant household that those who taught English best were the Christians, "the Goanese Jesuit fathers." Thus, Ismail was sent to both Christian and Muslim secondary schools. At home, he recalls, all his childhood reading was in English, books on trains being much in demand: "Everything then was railroads and steam engines." He liked the story of Cinderella and the exploits of Winnie-the-Pooh, "and that other one about the three bears, which was very popular with all of us." (He was the only son in a family of six daughters.) Later, at the age of eight or nine, he gave a public recitation of *The Charge of the Light Brigade*. "I loved the whole idea, the spirit of it, the valour." He read Shaw and Sheridan at school, and developed an appetite for anything written about the life and achievement of Benjamin Disraeli, the only Jew to have become Prime Minister of England. "I detect a similar spirit in you," one of his teachers declared, spurring his enthusiastic self-confidence.

ISMAIL MERCHANT, AGED 25, JUST BEFORE PRODUCTION OF *THE HOUSEHOLDER* IN 1961. "HE IS IN HIS FAMILY'S CROWDED APARTMENT IN NUL BAZAAR, BOMBAY," IVORY SAID. "WHERE THE DEBRIS FROM THE 1944 AMMUNITION SHIP EXPLOSION FELL THROUGH THE ROOF. THE APARTMENT WAS CROWDED—THOUGH COMPANIONABLY—DUE TO THE PRESENCE OF SIX ENERGETIC SISTERS. SOON AFTER THIS PICTURE WAS TAKEN, ISMAIL MOVED HIS WHOLE FAMILY TO LARGER QUARTERS ACROSS THE CITY, OVERLOOKING A LEAFY SQUARE."

The Romantic poets were part of the English curriculum. And the name E. M. Forster, author of *A Passage to India*, came up many times. "The attitude of our teachers towards Forster was very friendly, very encouraging," Merchant said. "He was considered as somebody sympathetic towards India, who felt for India. But Shakespeare was the pinnacle for us. Everything about Shakespeare had to be known. We studied the plays, in a sense, from an Indian viewpoint. We tried to understand them as they related to our own lives. *King Lear* came alive for me due partly to its parallels with Hindu mythology. Once, a Chinese theatre company visited school and performed a play which was based, I clearly remember, on a Shakespearean theme (though I forget now which one). Then, after 1947, Russian delegations came every year to India, and through them, one began to think in terms of other Western writers, Chekhov and Molière, for instance. In 1957, I acted the Suitor in an Urdu translation of Molière's *Scoundrel Scapin*."

Ismail Merchant first visited England in 1959, en route to New York, where he planned to take a degree in business administration. He stayed with his Bombay friend Kareem Samar, a law student with lodgings near Hampstead Heath, north London. The effect of the wooded, half-landscaped heath, with its necklace of ponds for bathing and angling, was immediate and entrancing. "It reminded me of an Indian hill station," Merchant said. "I thought, 'Why am I making a mistake and going to America when it's so beautiful here?' Looking back, I think my first real memory of England was, you might say, like an Impressionist painting of Hampstead Heath." The moment he arrived, Ismail announced he wished to make a pilgrimage to Oxford and Cambridge. "But Kareem said, 'It's a two-and-a-half-hour trip and you're only here for three days and I have my classes.' So, to my great disappointment, we didn't go."

As a child, Ismail knew only fellow Indians, "although my father was extremely close to an Anglo-Indian police inspector who called regularly at his shop." The first English person Merchant came to know well in India was the actress Jennifer Kendal, wife of the rising film star Shashi Kapoor, and then Jennifer's parents, Geoffrey and Laura Kendal, founders of the theatrical touring company Shakespeariana. "They didn't disappoint my expectations—not that I had any defined expectations. They were, above all, immensely friendly, and they had what I would term the right attitude." The experience of the Kendals in postwar India, as recorded in Geoffrey's diary, later became a starting point for the script of *Shakespeare Wallah*.

In London, after the completion of his first feature film, *The Householder*, which had its premiere in New York in October 1963, Merchant became acquainted, through his American partner James Ivory, with Howard Hodgkin, the English abstract painter, and Robert Skelton, then assistant curator of the Indian Department at the Victoria and Albert Museum in South Kensington. "They too were very much in the Indian mould. In fact, I've never met any Englishman who was unsympathetic to India, or didn't, let's say, have a broader vision about it. No, recently I did meet somebody. I was taken by a lawyer to a party at an exclusive club in London. 'Oh, really, how *wonderful*,' this gentleman said, with an extremely nasty twist, when I spoke about India. I retorted—I couldn't stop myself—that Indians speak better English than the English. And that absolutely burned him to death. He grew so annoyed. 'But,' I said, 'this is a fact of life!' And he grew even more upset. But then everything about him was a pretence."

⁂ ⁂ ⁂

IN 1966, between *Shakespeare Wallah* and their next film, *The Guru*, James Ivory and Ismail Merchant contacted Patrick Macrory, author of *Signal Catastrophe*, a newly published account of the retreat from Kabul. The retreat was among the blackest episodes in the history of the British army. In January 1842, a force of forty-five hundred British soldiers and some ten thousand camp followers were annihilated by Afghan warriors as they attempted to reach the safety of the garrison at Jalalabad. Ivory had read the diary of Lady Sale, heroine of the retreat, and thought that her personal story might possibly form the nucleus of a film. (Lady Sale had kept a diary before, during, and after her imprisonment by the Afghans.) "Ismail loved Afghanistan," Ivory said. "He was always telling people he was actually an Afghan and had Pathan blood. Quite untrue." The prospect of an epic film excited Merchant, according to Ivory. "But I just saw fifteen thousand of us, including the crew, marooned in those snowy ravines. . . ."

Invited to Macrory's home at Walton-on-the-Hill, Surrey, Ivory was introduced to his host's sixteen-year-old son, Richard, an amateur filmmaker of four years' standing. Talk of the retreat from Kabul was postponed, momentarily, while Ivory helped rewrite Richard's current script, an 8mm. horror movie, due to start shooting the next day. "Jim played the part of a vampire," Richard Macrory said. "He was very good, you could see the touches coming through. My father played another vampire. Like all filmmaking, it took a long, long time. At the end of the day, we dug a grave at the bottom of the garden and Jim lay down with a stake through his heart. When he finally got up, he said, 'Now I know what it's like being an actor. I'm never doing that again.' "

A month later, Merchant appeared on the Macrorys' doorstep. He brought as a fellow guest the star of *Shakespeare*

Wallah, Jennifer Kendal's young sister, Felicity. Having left the family company in India, Felicity was just beginning to make her way as an actress in England. "She was slightly cool," Richard Macrory said, "wondering perhaps what she had let herself in for in this untidy and slightly crazy Surrey household. My father had again prepared himself to talk about the book. But Ismail got in first. 'I gather Jim has made a movie with Richard,' he said. 'May I see it?' I showed the film, and he said, 'Well, I've got to make one now.' So we spent all that Sunday shooting a four-minute version of the retreat from Kabul with Ismail as an Afghan warrior, dressed in an old green-velvet curtain, and Felicity as an Afghan princess coming out of a tea chest. We made it on the common next to the house under the gaze of these rather prissy local people, who couldn't imagine what was going on. I was intrigued that Felicity, having been this very cool girl during lunch (she polished her nails and wouldn't talk to anyone), immediately came to life once we started filming. Afterwards, however, they still wouldn't talk about *Signal Catastrophe*, and that saga—of turning the book into a film—has gone on now for more than twenty-five years."

Later, Ivory was invited to watch Richard Macrory perform in the open-air Latin play produced each year by the classics master of Westminster School in Little Dean's Yard in the shadow of Westminster Abbey. "I was very proud that a real director, if not yet a famous one, was in the audience. And Jim, I believe, was intrigued by the oddity of it all. The boys were dressed in 1920s costumes, not togas; and the aristocrats spoke with upper-crust drawls, and the servants in Cockney. The classics master believed that P. G. Wodehouse's comedy of the clever servant was based on the Latin plays, and this play was very P. G. Wodehouse. Perhaps it sowed some seeds in Jim's mind."

RAQUEL WELCH, STAR OF *THE WILD PARTY* (1974), ON THE BLACK SATIN SHEET OF RICHARD MACRORY'S BED IN THE RIVERSIDE MISSION INN.

Sir Patrick Macrory, barrister and public servant, who died in 1993, and Richard Macrory, Professor of Environmental Law, Imperial College, London, subsequently became the first two successive chairmen of Merchant Ivory Productions, U.K. *The Wild Party*, which was shot at the Mission Inn, in Riverside, southern California, was the last Merchant Ivory film that Richard Macrory worked on. The film—the story of a silent-movie comedian's final, desperate attempt at a comeback—did not have a happy passage, with the star, Raquel Welch, famously falling out with her director. Macrory was a gofer in the art department. Having, for some reason, nowhere to stay at night, he slept on the set bed, covered with black satin sheets, on which, during working hours, Raquel Welch performed her somewhat forced love scenes. "At the end of the shoot," Macrory said, "I took the sheets and had them made into handkerchiefs and a tie. I arranged with my father years ago that I should wear that particular satin tie at his funeral—which of course I did, with some satisfaction."

⁂ ⁂ ⁂

JAMES IVORY was born in California and grew up, in the 1930s, in the town of Klamath Falls, in southern Oregon. His paternal grandfather, who was born in Cork, had emigrated to America in the 1870s. (Ivory is not, however, a common Irish name, and it is supposed that the Catholic Ivorys of Ireland originated in Protestant Scotland.) His maternal grandmother, however, claimed descent from the Virginia Randolphs—from John Rolfe and Pocahontas. "All Americans claiming F.F.V. ('First Families of Virginia') status insist on going back to John Rolfe and Pocahontas," Ivory said. "Winston Churchill claimed the same ancestry through his mother, Jennie Jerome, which is why he named his own son Randolph." As a boy, his favourite film image was, Ivory once said, a scene from *Belle Starr*, with Gene Tierney: a Yankee officer, cigar at a rakish angle, holding a candelabra to the lace curtains of a plantation house, then dashing the torch contemptuously through a windowpane.

England and the English only distantly interested young Ivory. "Everything then was focused on Ancient Egypt and pre-Revolutionary France, the American South, and the Wild West." Nor was England a place Ivory longed to visit. "Though I can remember certain grand events, the coronation of George VI, and, vaguely, the abdication scandal—perhaps only because Mrs. Simpson was an American. But I was certainly aware of English accents, because from time to time in a film, there would be an English butler or an English lord. I can remember, too, going to the movies in Klamath Falls to see the comedienne Beatrice Lillie. I can't recall whether on that occasion she tossed her long pearls over her shoulder. But I saw her later on Broadway, in *Auntie Mame*, and she certainly did then. Everyone was waiting for her to do it, and she did. Her pearls whirled round and round her body and fell at her feet—it was her famous trick and a showstopper."

The first English people Ivory met face-to-face were the relatives of a man who worked in the office of his father's lumber business. "We had dinner with them in a restaurant in Klamath Falls. There was a girl my own age who had been told that she ought to have a hamburger as a special American treat—and, I remember, she cut it up with a knife and fork, instead of picking it up in her hands. Did I tell her? I'm afraid perhaps I did. They were very very straight, salt-of-the-earth, middle-class people. Those were the first real English voices I listened to."

James Ivory's first authentic images of England were derived in part from books, A. A. Milne's *When We Were Very Young* and Kenneth Grahame's *The*

JAMES IVORY, DURING A HOT DELHI NIGHT, 1962.

BELLE STARR: "IN MOVIES OF THE 1930S AND 1940S," IVORY SAID, "PLANTATION HOUSES WERE MOST OFTEN TORCHED BY HOLDING A LIGHTED CANDLE TO THE 'PORTIERS,' AS MAMMY CALLED THEM IN *GONE WITH THE WIND*—HEAVY, FRINGED CURTAINS LIKE THE ONES SCARLETT MADE INTO A DRESS. THIS WOULD BE AFTER THE MARAUDERS—YANKEE OR BRITISH—CHARGED UP THE GRAND STAIRCASE ON THEIR HORSES, SLASHING AT THE BANISTER WITH THEIR SABRES."

Wind in the Willows. Indeed, he tried to convince the neighbourhood children that he himself was the creator of Ratty, Mole, and Mr. Toad. (Toad Hall, he later noted, was his first English stately home.) "And of course *Winnie-the-Pooh.* That was a big deal with American children, or a certain kind of American child." Ernest Shepard's illustrations for all three books lodged in his mind. The 1940 Hollywood version of *Swiss Family Robinson*, with Thomas Mitchell and Freddie Bartholomew, and Edna Best as the mother, also struck a particular chord. "The father couldn't bear the corruption and bad atmosphere of Regency London. So he put his family in a boat and sailed for the South Seas. Shipwrecked in a storm, they escaped to live an idyllic existence on an island, with the treasures of their London house, which they had saved, like the pianoforte and the silver candelabra—the only drawbacks were the enormous tarantula spiders, the hurricanes, and the typhoons."

Ivory loved humorous books about the English. "I fell on the floor when I read Stella Gibbons' *Cold Comfort Farm.*" P. G. Wodehouse, however, did not appeal. "Somehow, the idea of a butler didn't intrigue me at age twenty." In college he went through all Evelyn Waugh's prewar novels. "I think if I were to reread those books now, I would put them into proper perspective, but then I had no perspective. There were grand parties and grand houses, decrepit lords and drunken maharajas, society ladies and, I suppose, people with whom I could identify. Who were they, these unfortunate heroes, browbeaten third sons of whomever, who had no money, and were sent off, and landed in Africa? They seemed sophisticated, though, in a way that nothing I was reading about in the United States seemed sophisticated." Ivory later immersed himself in the satirical novels of Nancy Mitford—*The Pursuit of Love, Love in a Cold Climate,* and *The Blessing* ("though maybe three novels can't be called an immersion")—with their preference for France, and all things French, over the sometimes rather stuffy English.

"*SWISS FAMILY ROBINSON*—LIKE *BELLE STARR*—APPEALED TO MY BOYHOOD TASTE FOR DISASTERS," IVORY SAID. "HERE, AFTER THEIR SHIPWRECK, THE ROBINSON FAMILY SET UP CIVILIZED HOUSEKEEPING IN A TREE HOUSE ON A SOUTH SEA ISLAND, UNTIL THE TREE IS FELLED BY A HURRICANE AND ALL THE GRAND MAHOGANY FURNITURE FROM THEIR BERKELEY SQUARE MANSION IS SMASHED TO BITS."

TAKING the end of 1993 as a cut-off date, Ruth Prawer Jhabvala has written thirteen feature films for Merchant Ivory Productions (M.I.P.) and three of the company's television films—of which five in all have been set in England. At the time of writing, two other scripts, on Thomas Jefferson and Pablo Picasso, respectively, are awaiting production. In addition, Mrs. Jhabvala has exercised a light guiding influence on two or three of the four Merchant Ivory features not written by her. She has also worked on two unproduced M.I.P. projects: *A Lovely World*, a more-or-less finished sequel to *Shakespeare Wallah*, set in London during the Swinging Sixties; and *Three Continents*, a draft adaptation of her longest novel, spread across America, India, and England, and centred on a familiar Jhabvala theme, the mesmeric effect of charlatan gurus.

"My first thoughts on England, when we began to think of making a film in England, were not based on long observation," Ivory said. "They must have been semiformed by Ruth, by her knowledge and experience of the country. On the comic side, I remember early on our travelling miles to visit a grand English country house, a place I'd always been interested in, and then having the doors absolutely slammed in our faces, because it was the wrong day, or we'd come at the wrong time." Grand houses, open or closed, did not, however, feature prominently in Merchant Ivory's first completely English project. (The script of *A Lovely World* was delivered to the company Filmways, with whom Merchant Ivory Productions had an arrangement, but the film itself was never realized. "Ismail made the cardinal mistake, which he's never done again," Ivory said, "of handing over the script before he'd received the cheque. Filmways read it, and then said, 'No'—and wriggled out of paying Ruth as well. . . .")

Newly arrived from India, a young woman, Lizzie (Felicity Kendal), works hard to become a professional actress amid the razzmatazz of fashion conscious London. She craves Indian food and unconstrained Indian companionship, not prim English teas and the disapproval of the biscuit-dry aunt with whom she lodges. One scene has fashion designers Adrian and Adrienne chattering foolishly to a television interviewer on the steps of Waterloo Place, at the top of which stands the column to George IV's spendthrift brother, the Duke of York, dismissed Commander of the British Army. "Lizzie was full of optimism," James Ivory said. "To quote Jean Rhys, 'She rowed her little boat along.' But bad things did happen to her, and in the end, it seems, she's not going to be an actress." True love was to have been offered by a young man (Barry Foster), an ex-actor now happily employed on research for a cultural guidebook to England.

When Merchant and Ivory began making their first regular visits to London in the mid-1960s—*Shakespeare Wallah*, their "calling card," was a critical and popular success in England, and had a long run at London's leading art cinema, the Academy in Oxford Street—they stayed, as Ivory put it, "as and how we could." "We were really squatters. We had rented rooms, here and there, and we freeloaded off people, that's the only word for it, long-suffering people like Howard Hodgkin, in Holland Park, and Robert Skelton, further out of the city, whom I'd come to know through *The Delhi Way*, the documentary I made for the Asia Society of New York."

An invitation from Henry Herbert to lunch at Wilton House, near Salisbury, the home of his father, the sixteenth Earl of Pembroke, left a vivid impression. Wilton was the first ancient and truly grand English house that Ivory had looked over—as a welcome guest of the owner. They called on Ruth Jhabvala's friends John and Catherine Freeman in Hampstead. (John Freeman, former editor of the left-wing weekly the *New Statesman*, was appointed British High Commissioner to Delhi in the mid-1960s.) "Jock Murray, Ruth's London publisher, Osyth Leeston, her editor, Jock's wife and sons, were always a presence for us," Ivory said. Later, in the early 1980s, John Murray's famous offices at 50 Albemarle Street—where Lord Byron, a Murray author, was still a living presence—became a temporary refuge for the London outpost of Merchant Ivory Productions.

"I felt at home in England," Ivory said. "I felt a rapport with the people. At the same time, however, I always thought the English said to themselves—about me—'Oh, such a nice American, not like the others at all!' But Ruth never said anything bad about the English. Other than when doors were slammed in our faces, and she would say, 'You must expect that. That's the way they are.' "

SOME OF Ruth Prawer's forebears were born in Germany, and some travelled west to settle there during World War I and earlier—in flight from military conscription, it seems, in Russia and Poland. By the mid-1920s, her bourgeois family were settled German patriots, happy and assimilated. The adopted sanctuary of her Polish father and her Russian grandfather, and Ruth's own native home—from which they were all disinherited by the Nazis, beginning in 1933 and finally, irrevocably in 1939—was the industrial city of Cologne on the Rhine. Her father was a solicitor and her maternal grandfather the cantor in Cologne's biggest Jewish synagogue. Ruth Prawer was born in 1927. She learned English as well as Hebrew at school. "Everyone did—everyone knew they had to go somewhere." Just before the war, she emigrated to England with her parents and brother. "I stopped reading books in German. (Never, never again.) And I began almost at once to write in English. I read quantities of middlebrow English fiction, mixed up with better things—I read lots of Dickens, I loved reading Dickens." In 1951, she married and went to live in Delhi; and in 1975, she moved to Manhattan, returning regularly to India in the winter months. Of her three daughters, one lives in India, one in England, and one in the United States.

Ruth's husband, the architect C. S. H. Jhabvala, remembers his first trip to London from Bombay just after the war—the shabby, unpainted buildings and the suffusing smell of boiled cabbage. "But I cannot remember my first impression of England," Ruth Jhabvala said. "I was only twelve, my senses were hardly developed." What, then, was the first English book she read? She searched her memory—one of Richmal Crompton's "William" books, about the resilient, anarchic English schoolboy, William Brown, who, with fallen stockings and cap askew, planned adventures

RUTH PRAWER JHABVALA, JUHU BEACH, BOMBAY, DURING THE PERIOD OF MERCHANT IVORY'S FIRST FILM, *THE HOUSEHOLDER*.

and despised conformity, dull English middle-class conformity in particular. "I don't think I read the English children's classics when I was a young, but I read them much later, in India, to my own daughters."

When the Germans began to bomb Coventry, in the Midlands, Ruth Prawer was evacuated from there to the nearby town of Leamington Spa. She lodged with two maiden sisters and their caretaker father. In Leamington, she remembers, she first read *David Copperfield.* "It must, I think, have been my favourite Dickens." Later she moved to Hendon, north London, where her parents had settled. "I have very strong memories of the London blitz: living in shelters, going down to shelters in school hours, spending all night in shelters and coming out and wondering whether your house was still there, and passing others that weren't. I read an enormous amount at night in the London Underground—I remember my mother reading lots of Henry James, while I read *Gone With the Wind.* The film of *Gone With the Wind* came out in 1940, but I don't recall seeing it then, though I must have—I've seen it so many times since."

At first, Ruth Prawer never doubted that England was where she would spend the rest of her life. "I liked the English a lot," she said. "They were very, very kind. When I arrived, I really looked like a refugee, I was so thin and spindly. In London, there were a lot of refugees, so they weren't so popular. But in Coventry, there were very few, and in my school I was the only one—so I was most popular. I was, I guess, fairly well taught. Though I never really got much from teachers, or from anyone else, for that matter—I don't to this day. Besides English, I took French, Latin, history, and, I think, physics for my Higher Secondaries. I don't recall any set books, but the text I do remember from an earlier exam was, strangely enough, a book by Hugh Walpole called *The Cathedral.* Later, you were supposed to read rather more than set books—all the Shakespeare plays, not just one.

"London was my first choice of university. But I didn't make up my mind to go to university until the last second. I didn't know what I was going to do. But I benefited from it enormously. I spent so many years just reading, five in all, beginning in 1945, most of the time at the British Museum. I had only one teacher at university whom I thought was good, who made the text open up. He taught Middle English. So I became very fond of Langland and Chaucer. That one man wasn't a well-known scholar, he was just a humble lecturer. But he was the only one who seemed to have a passion for the task. As an undergraduate, I chose as my subject the Restoration dramatists, from whom I was absorbing an awful lot of dialogue. Later, when I did my M.A., I had a specialized subject which I thought up all by myself, 'The Short Story in England from 1700 to 1750.' But really there were no short stories in England then, just the briefest texts.

"My feeling for England will always be one of profound gratitude, I wouldn't be alive if it weren't for England. . . .Were 'doors slammed in my face'? No, not really. But then, I didn't attempt to open any, maybe that's why not. I was, you might say, a bit on the edge."

Catherine Freeman remembers her first meeting with Ruth Jhabvala in November 1958; it was just after she had moved with her first husband, the journalist Charles Wheeler, to the house next to the Jhabvalas in Rajpur Road, Old Delhi. "Down the garden path came this frail young woman, whose first words to me were, 'Have you brought any books?' I said, 'I've got a whole trunkload coming from England.' 'Thank God for that!' she said. When the trunk arrived, Ruth was round like a flash. I'd packed my own particular books, not absolute standards, to keep me going for a year—the Metaphysical poets, James Hogg's *Confessions of a Justified Sinner*, and of course, Jane Austen. But when she saw what was inside my tin trunk, this very gentle young woman stepped back with a sort of hiss of frustration and rage, and said, 'This is no good, I've got all these!'

"I chiefly remember Ruth lying down a great deal. The children were very small then, and Jhab was a superb what would now be called 'house-husband,' as well as a highly accomplished practising architect. There were dogs, a couple of servants, and Ruth, who had to lie down a lot—always fragile, but strong as steel, preserving herself for her real work. She was very fond of her Alsatian dogs. That was a little incongruous, this slight withdrawn figure and her large dogs. But there is a danger, talking about her being withdrawn, of suggesting that she was unfriendly. She wasn't at all. We used to lie on the bed together chatting and laughing. She always loved being made to laugh and she adored jokes and jokey situations. We often went together to strange gatherings, of expatriate ladies, and the like, and later, I'm sorry to say, we laughed till the tears came.

"Ruth loves Ismail's warmth and intuition. She loves to see life in others. She strikes me sometimes as a child at a window, always on the outside looking in at some great, warm room. She doesn't need to take part in the activity herself, she needs, in fact, to preserve herself from it. *Detachment* is a key word—religious detachment, the detachment of the artist, and, perhaps, the detachment of the heart as well."

THE ENGLISH have threaded a passage through the films of Merchant Ivory from the beginning. In *The Householder*, Prem (Shashi Kapoor), a freshly married young man from the lower middle class in Delhi, finds he must reconcile his uncertain aspirations with his daunting new responsibilities. He becomes friends with another young man, a spiritual American. This man embodies life's possibilities, but he cannot help Prem with the practical difficulties of coping with a pregnant wife and an overbearing mother-in-law. In one scene, still trying to solve his dilemma, Prem visits an eccentric house occupied by a self-absorbed old Englishman playing Beethoven on a wind-up gramophone. The film was made for $125,000 ("as and how we could"), and several actors were picked up from the amateur theatrical societies of Delhi. "The elderly Englishman was named Gardner Stanbridge," Ivory said. "He worked for the British Council, and one day he just came along and played the part."

THE HOUSEHOLDER (1963): GARDNER STANBRIDGE, MERCHANT IVORY'S FIRST AND, TO DATE, MOST ECCENTRIC ENGLISHMAN. IN THIS SCENE, HE EXPLAINS A CRACKPOT ART-HISTORICAL THEORY TO SHASHI KAPOOR, THE ANXIOUS NEWLYWED, WHILE BEETHOVEN'S "ODE TO JOY" PLAYS ON A GRAMOPHONE, RIGHT EDGE OF FRAME.

The English appear in greater force in *Shakespeare Wallah*. But, like the man with the gramophone, the English members of the Buckingham Players are also left-behind expatriates. The one exception is the spirited teenager Lizzie Buckingham (Felicity Kendal). She longs for something *different* (if only her spirited, irreverent boyfriend, Sanju), something indefinably better, and at the end, a tiny figure at the rail of a towering ocean liner, she sets off without responsibilities for a new life in "England"—the idea, as much as the country. ("Left to herself," Ivory said, "Lizzie would probably have stayed in India. It was mostly her parents who longed for her: they pushed her out.") Over the years, however, Lizzie's parents have slowly disinherited themselves from their native country. They have grown accustomed to India, comfortably accustomed, in fact, if only they could earn a satisfactory living. And yet, they are doubly exiled, from an England they have forgotten, and from an India that regards them, quite affectionately, as the tattered remnants of a departed era. Mrs. Bowen (Jennifer Kendal), the homely landlady of "Gleneagles," in a hill station to which the wandering company pays its annual pilgrimage, might have kept a boardinghouse in any timeless English seaside resort, except that one knows from Jennifer Kendal's every word and gesture that she will never quit the mock-Tudor familiarity of "British" Kasauli.

SHAKESPEARE WALLAH (1965): SHASHI KAPOOR AND FELICITY KENDAL. "I WAS INTRIGUED," RICHARD MACRORY SAID, "THAT FELICITY, HAVING BEEN THIS VERY COOL GIRL DURING LUNCH (SHE POLISHED HER NAILS AND WOULDN'T TALK TO ANYONE), IMMEDIATELY CAME TO LIFE ONCE WE STARTED FILMING."

Merchant Ivory's first truly English film—or at least the first of their films to be set entirely in England—was a fifty-four-minute 16mm. documentary commissioned by BBC Television in 1970, and entitled *Adventures of a Brown Man in Search of Civilization*. The subject was Nirad C. Chaudhuri, a tiny, loquacious, immensely energetic Indian, bubbling over with erudition and mischievous convictions. He dedicated his most famous book, *Autobiography of an Unknown Indian*, to the memory of the British Raj. Born in a village in East Bengal in 1897, Chaudhuri became, after years of ill-rewarded effort, an author and broadcaster—the enemy of all received wisdom, with an emphasis on Indian received wisdom. Merchant and Ivory were introduced to him in Delhi by his friends the Jhabvalas and by John and Catherine Freeman. In 1970, Chaudhuri, in customary high spirits, was staying in London and making pilgrimages to Oxford to carry out his research. He later settled permanently in Oxford, to the relief, no doubt, of his more hidebound countrymen.

Filming got under way in Oxford with the help of location scout Richard Macrory, by then an undergraduate at Christ Church. "Once, just before taking a shot, Jim asked if I'd walk along the street and feed Chaudhuri the odd question," Macrory said. "But I knew nothing about this distinguished man. He was then writing a book on Max Müller, the German-born British Sanskrit scholar, and in my ignorance I thought it was about Max Miller, the music-hall comedian. Added to which, Chaudhuri was half my height. He talked nonstop about English literature, and he was, needless to say, far better read than me. After the first take, I said to Jim, 'But I'm just nodding my head.' 'That's fine,' Ivory said, 'it's the effect he has on everybody.' We visited the churchyard where Max Müller was buried, near Magdalen College, and there is an incongruous long shot of me and Chaudhuri walking through some tall grass round the tombstones—this tall, languid figure, and alongside a homburg hat furiously popping up and down."

"By the time we made that movie," Ivory said, "I was into 'irony' with a big *I*. We took Chaudhuri to a Savile Row tailor, who measured him up while reminiscing about Rabindranath Tagore. Chaudhuri went along with this, very much so. He enjoyed putting on his velvet party coat with lace cuffs for our benefit. But I don't think he thought we were anything special. I felt, however, that I had to show him the feature film we'd just completed

NIRAD CHAUDHURI, A TINY, LOQUACIOUS, IMMENSELY ENERGETIC INDIAN, BUBBLING OVER WITH ERUDITION AND MISCHIEVOUS CONVICTIONS.

[*Bombay Talkie*, a melodrama set in the pumped-up world of the Indian film industry]. Afterwards, we were on an Underground train, and he leaned across the aisle and said—softly and incredulously, apropos the movie—'What *were* you thinking of?' And I don't know what I said. Nothing. I just couldn't say anything. 'What *were* you thinking of?' Just like that."

Sixteen years later, Ivory and his two partners went to lunch with Chaudhuri and his wife at their home in Oxford. "He absolutely exhausted us," Ivory said. "He sat next to Ruth and kept banging her on the shoulder to emphasize a point. By the end of the meal she was black-and-blue. We were invited to stay for tea as well. But we lied, we said we had to go to an important meeting. We drove away, parked the car, and then the three of us just collapsed, fell asleep for three hours, until it was time to go back.... In conversation, Chaudhuri doesn't need anybody to say anything. All he needs is a springboard. You could make a highly intelligent remark and he would have no interest in it; equally, you could say something utterly stupid and that wouldn't matter either. I think, however, if you really pinned him down, he would tell you something of great value and interest—but he would tell you such volumes, you'd wish you'd never asked.

"There's no doubt that Chaudhuri loves Western music and literature, and he certainly loves French wines, but whether he has an encyclopedic knowledge of them I don't know. He certainly has an encyclopedic knowledge of his favourite subject, which is India. Chaudhuri is, however, one of the happiest people I have ever known. I remember one scene in particular from the documentary. We filmed Chaudhuri in a taxi going round and round Trafalgar Square. He observes that England is now a country where nothing happens, that if you open an English newspaper there's nothing in it. If you open an Indian newspaper, there's too much. It's terrible and tragic and so on, but at least something's *happening* in India. In England, nothing's going on—and in a way I have to agree with that. I turn on breakfast television in London, just as I do in New York, and what do I invariably get by way of 'news'? A lot of political backbiting, men haranguing in the House of Commons; dull stuff from the City; and of course sports...."

Savages (1972), Merchant Ivory's next film, was an absurdist drama, with echoes of the work of the Surrealist Luis Buñuel, in which the rise and fall of civilisation (minus the Golden Age) was played out during a decadent party at a New York country mansion, in the grounds of which live a tribe of aboriginal Mud People. The co-scriptwriter, George Swift Trow, was, Ivory said, very fond of the English, and he inserted into the mayhem a doddery but imperturbable English couple, Sir Harry and Lady Cora, played by Neil Fitzgerald and Margaret

SIR HARRY (NEIL FITZGERALD, CENTRE) AND LADY CORA (MARGARET BREWSTER, RIGHT), DOUBTFUL PARTICIPANTS IN THE ORIENTAL HOKUM OF *SAVAGES* (1972).

AUTOBIOGRAPHY OF A PRINCESS (1975): THE PRINCESS (MADHUR JAFFREY) AND CYRIL SAHIB (JAMES MASON). MERCHANT IVORY'S FIRST COMPLETE, AND IN SOME WAYS NEVER-BETTERED CHARACTER STUDY OF A FRAYED ENGLISH GENTLEMAN.

Brewster. "I'm afraid that Fitzgerald, the old Irish stage actor, had trouble with his lines," Ivory said. "But I liked Margaret Brewster a lot. What a good sport she was to be plastered with mud on those cold mornings. That, I think, is very English, 'to be a good sport,' to put up with unspeakable physical sensations and not complain. Perhaps they were also good sports on the retreat from Kabul, but why did no one figure the danger? . . ."

Autobiography of a Princess (1975), which Ruth Jhabvala wrote back-to-back with her prize-winning novel *Heat and Dust*, is the story of a London tea party. The hostess is a divorced Indian princess (Madhur Jaffrey) and the single guest an elderly Englishman, Cyril Sahib, who was, long ago, companion-secretary to the princess's late father. The party is an annual event with its own rituals, but this year, the princess has acquired some old home movies of Indian princely life in hopes of jogging Cyril Sahib's memory. She would like him to write the biography of her father, a disarming rogue disgraced, finally, by a sexual indiscretion at the Savoy Hotel. No Merchant Ivory film is complete without a meal, and here, with typical incongruity, the teatime fare includes *samosas*, the fried Indian finger food, and a Fuller's cake, the most famous of English bought cakes, with its halved walnuts and incomparable powdery white icing. The old secretary, however, cannot be tempted with savouries and sweetmeats.

Cyril Sahib, played with absolute precision by a weary, hunched James Mason, his black suit set off by a dun-coloured cardigan, is Merchant Ivory's first complete, and in some ways never-bettered, character study of a frayed English gentleman. Cyril had led a disappointed life, the lines of which can be read on his face. But he is in no sense self-pitying. He is expert in not giving offence. He has his own book to write, the biography of an exemplary English imperial administrator, who, before dying of cholera, collected among other things the traditional songs of Orissa. But the end of the book seems never in sight. Cyril loved India—continues to love it, in fact—but the country finally destroyed him by refusing to let him go. He is a sympathetic, unforgettable human being who inhabits a wholly believable off-screen world. When he talks about the past, he brings it effortlessly before our eyes. He chooses his words with care. One could not imagine him gesticulating at meal-times, or asserting some dogmatic point about the wickedness of India by jabbing a finger into his neighbour's ribs.

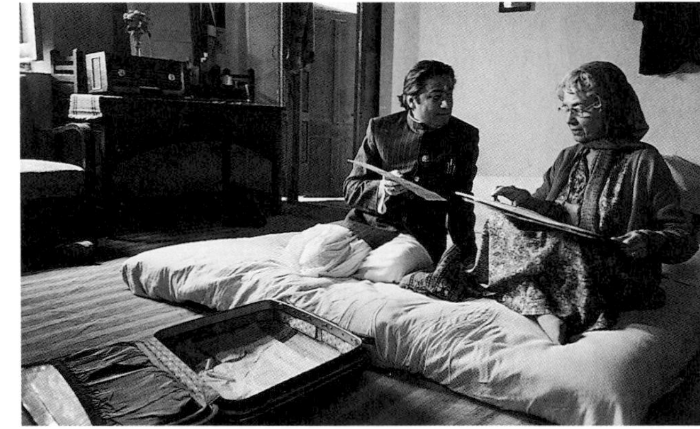

HULLABALOO OVER GEORGIE AND BONNIE'S PICTURES (1978): LADY GWYNETH MCLAREN PUGH (PEGGY ASHCROFT) EXAMINES THE "MOST PRECIOUS AND PRIVATE COLLECTION" OF ART DEALER SHRI NARAIN (SAEED JAFFREY). "SOME OF THE PICTURES WERE PORNOGRAPHIC," IVORY SAID, "AND WERE HELD BACK BY THEIR EMBARRASSED OWNER. BUT LADY GEE, UNFAZED BY THEIR CONTENT AND ALWAYS RELENTLESS IN HER SEARCH FOR ARTISTIC AND HISTORIC VALUE, SNATCHED THEM UP AND GAVE THEM A CRITICAL ONCE-OVER."

The single location of *Autobiography of a Princess* was a flat behind Holland Park Underground station in Kensington. It was owned by a russophile named Johnny Stuart and filled with Russian art which had to be put safely to one side. "It was a very good mid-nineteenth-century room with French windows opening on to an iron balcony," Ivory said. "The art direction was a concoction, since the Indian royal ladies we knew lived in far grander style. They'd take flats at Claridge's, for a year, and then turn everything upside down. We filmed at another location for one of the documentary sequences, a substantial, unattractive Edwardian house at Ascot, in Berkshire, owned by the Maharaja of Jaipur. Lindy Dufferin, the Marchioness of Dufferin and Ava, did an unscripted interview with the Maharani of Jaipur and her son, seated in a cold, very un-Indian room beneath an immense full-length portrait of the Maharani by the society painter Pietro Annigoni."

If Cyril Sahib was the epitome of the Englishman entranced and destroyed by too many years in India, then Lady Gwyneth McLaren Pugh, "Lady Gee"—Merchant Ivory's next full-length English character study, in *Hullabaloo Over Georgie and Bonnie's Pictures* (1978)—was the epitome of an Englishwoman capable of standing up to everything that India could throw at her. *Hullabaloo*, filmed at the vast Art Deco palace of the Maharaja of Jodhpur, is the story of the comic battle for the Tasveer Collection, a priceless cache of Indian miniature paintings, fought between an unscrupulous young American (Larry Pine) and an indomitable Englishwoman whose late husband had been aide-de-camp to the Viceroy. Lady Gee (Peggy Ashcroft) was, Ivory said, an echo of Dr. Mildred Archer, curator of prints and drawings at the India Office Library in London, who had lived in India from 1934 to 1947 and was the "great guru" of Indian paintings, notably those painted for the British in India, called "Company" pictures.

Lady Gee was also, and perhaps more closely, based on another formidable Englishwoman, Penelope Betjeman, widow of the Poet Laureate. John Betjeman was a Murray author, and both Ruth Jhabvala and Peggy Ashcroft knew Penelope well. "She was very opinionated and talked in a great loud voice," Ivory said. "Henry Herbert once wanted to make a film of six English eccentrics, and she was one of them. The last time I met her was at John Murray's, when we were there in the office prior to the filming of *Heat and Dust* in 1982. She was just back from the Himalayas, where she had heard rumours of a human sacrifice—and she was desperately disappointed not to have been present for the sacrifice, if it was true. Penelope Betjeman was a great friend of Elizabeth, wife of the author Bruce Chatwin, and they would often go off together on these long treks—just like Lady Gee in her VW van. Sometimes Bruce would be invited, but he never really wanted to go to the tops of mountains with these groups of powerful women. He much preferred deserts, I think."

QUARTET (1981): H. J. HEIDLER (ALAN BATES), OUTFITTED FOR THE HUNT, WITH HIS VICTIM MARYA (ISABELLE ADJANI). HEIDLER WAS THE KIND OF INSOLENT ENGLISHMAN THAT AS A CLASS THOMAS JEFFERSON, WRITING IN 1787, BELIEVED HAD TO BE "KICKED INTO COMMON GOOD MANNERS."

A different and less admirable "Englishman abroad," the

philanderer H. J. Heidler, played by Alan Bates, appears in Merchant Ivory's adaptation of Jean Rhys' novel *Quartet* (1981). Heidler lives in an elegant studio apartment in Paris with his wife, Lois (Maggie Smith). He takes breakfast in a silk dressing gown and ostentatiously shakes out a copy of the morning paper; and in the evening, he affects a Russian fur hat, at an angle, when going to be entertained at the cabaret. (Lady Gee, with her floppy denim explorer's hat, set no great store by the clothes she wore; and in the evening in the palace entertained herself with a game of patience at a little round table.) The year of *Quartet* is 1927, and Lois, a lady painter, has long since learned the necessary art of keeping up public appearances when as usual things go messily wrong with the latest of H.J.'s broken-winged protégées, Marya, played by Isabelle Adjani. The central mystery of the film is, perhaps, how Lois Heidler could have loved such a spineless man as H. J. "You have no sympathy for Lois loving such a man as Heidler—or for that matter, Marya," Ivory said, "unless you are so broad-minded about love that you can accept and forgive any kind of bad behaviour."

QUARTET: THE OVERBEARING HEIDLER (ALAN BATES), ATTENDED BY HIS WIFE, LOIS (MAGGIE SMITH), AND HIS MISTRESS, MARYA (ISABELLE ADJANI).

In the 1920s, an Englishman or American could make a fixed income go a long way in Paris. "It is hard to say exactly what Heidler did," Ivory said. "He was a critic, he wrote about art, and he 'helped people.' He would discover artists, or think he discovered artists, and he would put them together with someone who would write about them, or with a gallery which would exhibit their work. If you were after hedonistic pleasures in the 1920s, you'd go to Paris. And if you had money, you would have many hedonistic pleasures. In those days, the pound was supreme. You could afford to buy art, and you could live like a king. And that's what Heidler did—rather as Ford Madox Ford did, on whom Jean Rhys mostly based her portrait of this, the first of Merchant Ivory's 'devilish' Englishmen."

WHEN I took the bus from Boston to New Ipswich, New Hampshire, in October 1978, to visit the set of *The Europeans*, I had no idea what to expect, whom I would meet, or if anything would result from my conversation with Ruth Jhabvala. The day of my visit was a Friday, and Ismail, having commandeered the kitchen of the motel where the production was based, was showing a lowly assistant how to pull the skin off a chicken leg. He was preparing the crew's Friday night feast. And he was, I remember, upset that I would not stay the night and taste his cooking. If my family expected me home so soon, why had I not brought my family with me? They would have enjoyed the beautiful autumn day ("See, just a sprinkling of sand on the road and we are in the nineteenth century"), and the dignified old white-painted house and its neighbouring cottage ("Just as Henry James described it"), and the gazebo at the top of a gentle, wooded slope ("Come, I will show you"). "Look at the pond. See, there are Eugenia and Mr. Acton, arm in arm on the path. What could be more delightful?" He shook his head in disbelief at the customs of the English. What folly to come away so soon!

I conducted the interview with Ruth Jhabvala. My chief memory of her motel room is of its emptiness. It seemed

SAUNDERS (PATRICK GODFREY), THE SHORT-TEMPERED ENGLISH DOCTOR OF *HEAT AND DUST* (1983), TAKING ACTION AGAINST A POOR INDIAN FAMILY. THE FAMILY HAD ENCOURAGED ONE OF THEIR WOMEN TO HAVE AN ABORTION. GODFREY LATER PLAYED THE SUPERIOR REVEREND EAGER IN *A ROOM WITH A VIEW*; SIMCOX, THE DISAPPROVING WEST COUNTRY BUTLER IN *MAURICE*; AND SPENCER, AN ILL-BRED HOUSE-GUEST IN *THE REMAINS OF THE DAY*.

to contain nothing except, on the table between us, a tattered paperback edition of *The Europeans*. Ruth was courteous and answered my questions as best she could. Did she try to sit down to write every day? She didn't "try," she sat down! (Her voice rose for a moment.) As she grew older, she said, she felt increasing sympathy for Henry James. His friend Edith Wharton was forever swooping down in her large car and carrying him off to parties. He preferred to keep to his desk—and Ruth did too. The interview was duly written up, and Penelope Houston gave it, out of fondness for Ismail Merchant and Henry James, a more than usually generous allowance of pictures. Time passed and Ismail again materialized in our quarters—though I cannot remember on what pretext this time, perhaps to tell us how Jim and Ruth were going to conjure up a miraculous film in Manhattan from a few unpublished pages of Jane Austen's childish fancy. . . .

A year or two later, Ismail invited me to Hyderabad during the shooting of *Heat and Dust*. It would give immediacy to the last chapter of a book I was preparing on the first twenty-one years of Merchant Ivory Productions. One scene, in particular, remains vividly in my mind from the filming of *Heat and Dust*. The story, it will be remembered, unravels the life of a young Englishwoman, Olivia (Greta Scacchi), married to a dull District Collector consigned in the 1920s to the Civil Lines of the Princely State of Khatm (meaning "finished, all done"). She is seduced by the state's roguish Nawab (Shashi Kapoor, never more serpentlike), and, freed from everything she has known—her "Englishness" and her responsibilities—she discovers that she is her own mature person with her own mysterious destiny. The scene I remember was a tea party—a picnic, this time, on a raised lakeside promontory—at which the Nawab entertains a group of his English friends, including Olivia, with a delightful, leisurely game of musical cushions. The setting in the parched red-brown middle of nowhere was unforgettable, and the lake was made a work of art, courtesy of Merchant Ivory, by the reflection on its surface of a tiny pastel-coloured shrine they had built on the shore. The Nawab's manners were feminine in their delicacy; his concern for his guests was complete ("Here, please," he indicated to Olivia, "take the last cushion")—no wonder these clenched English people, so far from home, could do nothing but lie on the carpet among the cushions and give themselves over to joyful laughter.

MUSICAL CUSHIONS: HARRY (NICKOLAS GRACE), OLIVIA (GRETA SCACCHI), AND THE NAWAB (SHASHI KAPOOR).

A Room with a View

MR. EMERSON:

Make my boy realize that by the side of the everlasting Why there is a yes! A Yes and a Yes.

This inflated oratory brings LUCY *back to earth. She adopts a tone of solid, suburban common sense.*

LUCY:

Has your son no particular hobby? I generally forget my worries at the piano; and collecting stamps did no end of good to Freddy, my brother . . .

—Shooting script, scene 22,
in the Church of Santa Croce

Miss Lavish (Judi Dench) offers the self-effacing Miss Bartlett (Maggie Smith) the protection of a mackintosh square.

Pages 32–33: Lucy (Helena Bonham Carter), Minnie (Mia Fothergill), and Freddy (Rupert Graves) play bumble-puppy; Mrs. Honeychurch (Rosemary Leach) and the Reverend Beebe (Simon Callow) observe.

On a hillside near Maiano, outside Florence, in the opening section of *A Room with a View* (1985), the first of Merchant Ivory's three films adapted from the novels of E. M. Forster, Eleanor Lavish, a romantic novelist, produces two mackintosh squares and lays them with a flourish on the dry ground. The English prepare to take a picnic. Miss Lavish (Judi Dench) settles herself on one square, and Miss Charlotte Bartlett (Maggie Smith), chaperon to her cousin Lucy (Helena Bonham Carter), insists that her charge occupy the other. "The ground will do for me," Charlotte says. "I have not had rheumatism for years, and if I do feel a twinge, I shall stand up." The two older women continue to gossip until Miss Lavish makes a sign with her eyes—she cannot say more in Lucy's presence.

Charlotte clears her throat ("No, no, don't be alarmed; this isn't a cold. . . ."), and Lucy, taking the hint, wanders off to look for Mr. Arthur Beebe, a cheerful and perspicacious clergyman, who is having a separate picnic with Mr. Emerson, a retired journalist, and the Reverend Mr. Eager, Chaplain of the Anglican Church in Florence. Mr. Emerson's son, George (Julian Sands), has just toppled out of an olive tree, while proclaiming his creed ("Beauty—Joy—Love!") at the top of his voice, to the entire Arno Valley. Joining a line of decisive Merchant Ivory girls, Lucy seizes the initiative. She forgets Mr. Beebe and approaches the handsome sleepy-eyed coachman who brought them from Florence. He directs her to George, standing alone in a field of grain, gazing at the view. The awkward young Englishman turns, forgets, for a second, the "everlasting Why," wades through the barley and takes Lucy in his arms. Charlotte, who has come running to the rescue, calls out in impotent distress.

Gathered on the Tuscan hill, for the occasion of this famous kiss, is a vivid assortment of English comic types. Charlotte Bartlett is suffocated by a sense of responsibility. Continental travel entails guarding against cheats, not placing oneself under an obligation to strangers, and being compelled to eat meat which, one suspects, has already been boiled for soup. Everything, in short, is a worry. Miss Lavish, on the other hand, bares her breast to experience. She inhales the rich air of Florence with a contented sigh. Her favourite flower is not the "delightful" violet. She prefers "something wilder, bolder—the reckless rose, the tempestuous tulip." She abhors Baedeker. And had she found herself in the Himalayas, she would doubtless have gone in search of adventures, if not perhaps a human sacrifice.

Of the two clergymen, the know-it-all Mr. Eager (Patrick Godfrey) is conceited and spiteful, his pursed lips and bushy whiskers as precise and angular as his hat, while the enquiring Mr. Beebe

(Simon Callow) is the soul of energetic, muscular Christianity, and, as he will prove back in England, when he strips off his constraining clerical garb and leaps into the Sacred Lake, game for almost anything. Mr. Emerson, having been a journalist, talks straight, yet everything he says is touched by a peculiarly trusting nonconformity. All these people are deliberate caricatures, illuminating the human dilemma of the central and somewhat more natural characters, George and Lucy. But they are living, affectionate caricatures, executed with the dexterity and humour with which, in the years of the Hollywood studio system, such expatriates as Eric Blore and Sir C. Aubrey Smith used to impersonate the English—butlers, noblemen, foolish old buffers—for the amusement of America and the world.

⁂

"IN AMERICA, when I became interested in India," James Ivory said, "the only available Indian novel, apart from Ruth's stories, was *A Passage to India*. The work of Forster's friend J. R. Ackerley hadn't been published yet, or if it had come out in America, it was forgotten. I read *A Passage to India* in 1958, followed by the other Forster novels in the Sixties. I didn't like *Howards End* the first time I read it. I couldn't really get it. It didn't mean anything to me, as it does to so many people. I read *A Room with a View* and *Where Angels Fear to Tread* because of their Italian background. [Ivory's M.A. thesis film dealt with artistic representations of Venice.] And I read *Maurice* when it was first published, after Forster's death, in 1971. The odd thing about Forster, as far as I was concerned, was that I never had a very clear sense of the stories. I could remember some of his characters, everyone in *A Passage to India*, for example, and, of course, Cecil Vyse from *A Room with a View*, but by no means all of them. And perhaps that's how it should be, since Forster didn't think his plots were anything, or in any sense important; it was everything else that was significant."

MISS CHARLOTTE BARTLETT (MAGGIE SMITH).

In 1961, en route to India, where he was to begin work on *The Householder*, Ivory made a stopover in England. He had become acquainted in New York with several "official" Indians, one of whom—"he had gotten to know Forster and had set himself up as 'Morgan's Friend' (though with what justification I cannot tell)"—gave him a letter of introduction. "He wrote to Forster to say that this young American, who had made a very nice documentary, *The Sword and the Flute*, and was making another film in Delhi, and so on, would like to see you and could you invite him to Cambridge." The famous novelist obliged. But on the morning of the appointed day, with Ivory already in his best clothes, a letter arrived saying that Forster, then aged eighty-two, was feeling unwell. "I was relieved in a way," Ivory said. "What would I have said to him, and what could he have wanted to say to me? It would have been like meeting Nirad Chaudhuri. I would have just sat there, looking at him. He always sat with his knees together, just so; and that's how I would have sat, on one of those lawn chairs in the King's College quadrangle. He was then an old man; and he would reread his novels, and say such things as, 'This is very good,' or 'This is not bad at all.' Really, what could I have added?"

Lucy's engagement party, Emmetts, Kent. The festive marquee is a standard fixture of the frequently damp English summer. But, for Ivory, these party tents hold a deeper meaning. "They are sometimes a convenient way to define your guests' social standing. Important people are shown into one tent, less grand ones into another—further down the lawn. No one seems to complain about this, it is only right and natural."

George Emerson declares his creed.

On first seeing Lucy: The Emersons (Julian Sands and Denholm Elliott) in the dining room of the Pensione Bertolini.

THREE MERCHANT IVORY VETERANS ON A HILLTOP ABOVE FLORENCE. "THE COMPOSITION RESEMBLES A *SACRA CONVERSAZIONE*," IVORY SAID. "THE SWEET-NATURED BUT AGNOSTIC MR. EMERSON (DENHOLM ELLIOTT), CENTRE, IS FLANKED BY CLERGYMEN OF CONTRASTING TEMPERAMENTS. AT LEFT IS A SOMEWHAT LOUNGING MR. BEEBE (SIMON CALLOW), WHO, AS PART OF HIS CREED, WELCOMES LIFE'S UNEXPECTED FELICITIES; AT RIGHT IS THE STIFF-BACKED MR. EAGER (PATRICK GODFREY)—FOREVER DENYING THEM."

THE PIAZZA DELLA SANTISSIMA ANNUNZIATA: ENGLISH LADIES PREPARE FOR ADVENTURE.

The Piazza della Signoria: Italian passions, English bewilderment.

❧ ❧ ❧

AFTER THE incident on the hillside, Charlotte Bartlett whisks Lucy home to her mother, Mrs. Honeychurch, at Windy Corner, in Summer Street, Surrey. There, Lucy allows herself to become engaged to Cecil Vyse. "Lucy's Fiasco" (Daniel Day Lewis) is a fastidious black stick insect, his white shirt has an enormously high collar, and his pince-nez is always in need of the most delicate readjustment. Cecil is a magnificent snob, and it is his snobbery that undoes him. On a visit to the National Gallery in Trafalgar Square, he bumps into the Emersons. They fall into conversation while admiring the immense, close-packed drama of Uccello's *The Battle of San Romano*. It transpires that father and son are looking for a house to rent in the country. Cecil thinks it would be amusing, and deliciously appropriate, to put these two commonplace people in touch with Sir Harry Otway, the landlord of Summer Street, whom Cecil regards as the vulgar embodiment of everything he dislikes about country life and country values.

Later, strolling through the woods at Windy Corner, Cecil is thunderstruck to come upon George, Lucy's brother, Freddy, and Mr. Beebe, Summer Street's new vicar, cavorting naked in a pond. The scene is richly comic. The men are having too much fun to be seriously embarrassed, and Cecil's companions, Lucy and Mrs. Honeychurch, can barely contain their giggles. Cutting a manly path through the bracken with his walking stick, Cecil leads the ladies to safety. In the excitement, all Mr. Beebe's clothes have been tossed in the water. How he got home we never know. It's at that moment, perhaps, that Lucy realizes, although she will not acknowledge it, that her destiny does not lie with Cecil.

LUCY'S FIASCO (DANIEL DAY LEWIS).

❧ ❧ ❧

"YOU KNOW Kent and Surrey," Ismail said to me one autumn evening in 1984, after we had bumped into each other on the pavement outside the Haymarket Theatre in the West End. "You must help us find the Sacred Lake." I agreed and invited Jim and Ismail to my family's home, Foxwold, near the village of Brasted, in Kent, not far from the Surrey border. After lunch, we set off on foot to inspect several beautiful, but, as they pointed out, tramping through the nettles and mud, hardly accessible ponds. In the woods not far from Foxwold, on the edge of what used to be an orchard meadow, was a disused sunken garden overhung by a large beech tree. Ismail brightened. He had found a place where his art director could put a pond. It would do splendidly. "But," he added as an afterthought, "the pond is no use without the house."

Lucy Honeychurch (Helena Bonham Carter) safe at home.

Freddy (Rupert Graves) prepares to sing a comic song. Mrs. Honeychurch (Rosemary Leach) and Lucy (Helena Bonham Carter) are all set to encourage him, but Cecil Vyse (Daniel Day Lewis) winces with displeasure.

Chiddingstone, Kent: Lucy stands up to her fault-finding fiancé.

Left: Mr. Beebe (Simon Callow) and Freddy (Rupert Graves) on the drive at Windy Corner. The trees behind no longer stand.

In the Sacred Lake: Freddy (Rupert Graves), the Reverend Beebe (Simon Callow), and George (Julian Sands).

Beside the Sacred Lake: Cecil dislodges his pince-nez.

KISSED—OR INSULTED—A SECOND TIME.

Thus Foxwold, a large, many-gabled house built by a London solicitor, Horace Pym, in 1883, became Windy Corner. A cream-coloured polythene skin was draped over the sunken garden; water was run in from a tap in the woods; ferns and potted bulrushes appeared round the edge; buoyant staging covered with turf made the outline irregular; and a pump was installed to heat the water to the temperature of a tepid bath. The pond was dark, mysterious, and idyllic; and after the film crew had departed, it was a nostalgic reminder of their presence, even when the staging rotted and the water became thick and black with beech leaves. Two years later, on the night of October 16, 1987, a hurricane blew up the English Channel and cut a swath through the southeast of England, decimating the trees of Kent, and destroying nearly eighty acres of woodland at Foxwold. The beech over the Sacred Lake came up by its roots and a branch pierced the polythene skin.

"When we 'set fire' to a room at the Umaid Bhavan Palace," Ivory once said, "for the climactic scene [of *Hullabaloo Over Georgie and Bonnie's Pictures*] in which the miniature paintings apparently burn up, and we damaged a stone window frame, life seemed to imitate art when the real Maharani waved away our expressions of dismay and sorrow with a supreme gesture of aristocratic nonchalance, and, as one who has a thousand other windows, said that it didn't matter, that a little plaster of Paris would fix up everything. But it did matter, for we left that palace, finished only in 1946, worse than when we found it. It had been in pristine condition, and a film crew, headed by an American director as intent on making his film, and the cost be damned, as the American collector of the story was intent on rifling his host's storeroom, became the first barbaric invasion to descend on one of India's greatest palaces. It was only a chip lost, but we knocked that chip out as surely as if we had fired a cannon at the ramparts." To which Ismail Merchant replied: "Oh, that's all nonsense. We didn't leave the palace worse than we found it We made our film there and just enhanced it."

The Sacred Lake has not survived; it is now, in fact, an elephants' graveyard of uprooted tree stumps. And bits and pieces were knocked off Horace Pym's house: the sundial on which Cecil leans, during the tea party at which Charlotte Bartlett cannot find the correct change for the cabman, was given a rejuvenating coat of bleach and has yet to regain the pleasant patina of age; and the stucco between the half-timbering on the gables, which received a light water-soluble yellow wash (Windy Corner was, after all, as far as the story is concerned, a relatively new house), still gleams with unnatural brightness as one approaches the house up the drive. On the other hand, two thick blue velvet curtains, left behind by the art department, still hang from an improvised plywood surround across the arch at the bottom of the stairs—perfect for amateur theatricals and the exclusion of draughts.

What *A Room with a View* preserves, however, is far more significant: the branch from which George swings for a second over the Sacred Lake; the view of the woods in full leaf seen at the end of the tennis court where Lucy, Freddy, and young Minnie Beebe play bumble-puppy; the rhododendron beneath which George kisses Lucy for the second time; the verdant path down which Cecil leads the ladies before their encounter with the naked men—all that has gone, changed beyond recognition by the wind, and now only exists, like the fragmentary scenes of Indian royal life in *Autobiography of a Princess*, in the interstices of a touching comic film about the duties of the human heart.

A ROOM WITH A VIEW.

Gazetteer

The Italian sequences of *A Room with a View* were filmed in Florence, notably in the **Piazza della Signoria** and in the church of **Santa Croce**. A private villa in the town of Maiano was used for the interiors of the Pensione Bertolini; and the Hotel-Pensione **Quisisana e Ponte Vecchio**, Lungarno Archibusieri, provided the room (22) out of whose window there was, regrettably, no view. The Quisisana, where crew members stayed during the Italian production period, was badly damaged by a bomb that exploded against a wall of the Uffizi in May 1993. The carriages bearing Mr. Eager and his party to the hillside picnic were photographed on the road from **Florence to Fiesole** and passed the Villa I Tatti of Bernard Berenson.

The English sequences were chiefly filmed in and around **Sevenoaks**, Kent, a few miles north of the town of Tonbridge where E. M. Forster attended secondary school. The garden and interiors of Windy Corner, and the scenes at the Sacred Lake, were all photographed at **Foxwold**, a private house near Brasted, on the A25 between Westerham and Sevenoaks. Sir Harry Otway's garden party was set in the National Trust garden at **Emmetts**, near Ide Hill, the boyhood house of Forster's Cambridge contemporary and fellow writer Percy Lubbock. The fourteenth-century **Saint Mary's Church**, in the village of Chiddingstone, on the River Eden near Penshurst, served as the exterior of Mr. Beebe's church; **Chiddingstone Village Hall** was the Emersons' home, and a room in **Saint Mary's Rectory** was the sitting room in which George's father finally speaks his mind. In London, the **Estonian Legation** (now the Estonian Embassy), Queensway, was the residence of the indomitable Miss Alans; and the **Linley Sambourne House**, Kensington, provided the rich Victorian backdrop for the musical evening of the complacent Mrs. Vyse.

The damage caused to the woods of Kent by the hurricane of October 1987 has been softened by replanting and natural regeneration, and many walks can now be taken near Brasted, at Toy's Hill and Ide Hill, in particular (see "Walking for Pleasure," a pack of eight circular walks using Definitive Rights of Way, Tel. Sevenoaks D.C., 01732 741222). The following houses and gardens should also be of particular interest.

Emmetts: 3 miles southwest of Sevenoaks, open April to October, certain days, Tel. 01732 750367. This five-acre garden, the highest in Kent, is notable for the variety of its trees (including a hundred-foot redwood), its autumn foliage, and an immense bank of May bluebells.

Chiddingstone Castle: off the B2027, 3 miles east of Edenbridge, open April to October, certain days, Tel. 01892 870347. A seventeenth-century mansion with nineteenth-century Gothic Revival trimmings, owned between 1955 and 1977 by the connoisseur Denys Eyre Bower, a collector of Japanese art and Stuart mementoes.

Chartwell: off the B2026, 2 miles south of Westerham, open April to November, certain days, Tel. 01732 866368. This, the much-visited home of Winston Churchill, from 1924 until his death in 1965, is a pleasantly informal mine of Churchilliana: documents, amateur paintings, civil and military decorations, uniforms, hats, audio recordings, signed photographs of everyone who was anyone. Churchill brushed against E. M. Forster in a Belfast hotel during a particularly fraught moment of Irish history in 1912. The politician was on his way to address the

Ulster Liberal Association on new Home Rule proposals. Forster, not subsequently among the great man's admirers, noted that Churchill looked "very pale like some underground vegetable." According to his biographer, P. N. Furbank, the novelist none the less "valiantly raised his cap."

Knole: A225 in Sevenoaks, open April to October, certain days, Tel. 01732 450608. Surrounded by a thousand acres of deer parkland, this vast, mysterious "calendar" house (365 rooms, 52 staircases, 7 courtyards) was the gift of Elizabeth I to the Sackville family and contains, among many treasures, the world's pre-eminent collection of seventeenth-century English furniture.

Sissinghurst Garden: off the A262, 2 miles northeast of Cranbrook, open April to mid-October, certain days, Tel. 01580 712850. When the novelist and poet Vita Sackville-West left her beloved Knole in 1930, she and her husband, the diplomat Harold Nicolson, began the creation of this, the most famous literary garden in England. (On one occasion, Nicolson and Forster crossed swords in the *Spectator*, over the propriety of several English writers, including W. H. Auden and Christopher Isherwood, having retired to the United States at the start of World War II.)

Charleston Farmhouse: off the A27, 6 miles east of Lewes, East Sussex, open April to October, certain days, Tel. 01323 811265. The country home from 1916 of Vanessa Bell, the artist sister of Virginia Woolf, and now a much-decorated, though essentially unpretentious shrine to the Bloomsbury Group. E. M. Forster was one of many visitors. Subsequently occupied by the painter Duncan Grant.

And in London, the **Linley Sambourne House**, 18 Stafford Terrace, W8, open March to October, Sunday afternoons, Tel. 0181-994 1019. A uniquely well-preserved Victorian house, owned from 1874 to 1910 by the artist and *Punch* cartoonist whose name it bears. Sambourne's descendants, including the theatre designer Oliver Messel, arranged the furniture, pictures, and decorations exactly as in the 1890s.

Tourist Information Centre/Accommodation: Buckhurst Lane, Sevenoaks, Kent TN13 1LQ; Tel. 01732 450305. **Travel London–Sevenoaks**: Trains from Charing Cross, Victoria, and Cannon Street stations. By car, M25, A21, A25.

MAURICE

LASKER JONES [*an American hypnotist*]:
I needn't remind you that your sort were once put to death in England. I would advise you to live in some country—France, Italy—where homosexuality is no longer criminal.

MAURICE:
Will it ever be like that in England?

LASKER JONES:
England has always been disinclined to accept human nature.

—SHOOTING SCRIPT, SCENE 142,
A WIGMORE STREET CONSULTING ROOM

Unaware of what they are about to encounter.

Pages 52–53: There! Everything is clear, and need never be spoken of again.

If Cecil Vyse, of *A Room with a View*, was a snob, his adoring mother was a greater one. Mrs. Vyse hosts a musical evening to display Cecil's fiancée to her London circle; and Lucy Honeychurch, who plays Schubert (not her customary, tempestuous Beethoven), makes exactly the right impression. Gazing up at her son, her bosom swelling with pride, Mrs. Vyse extols her future daughter-in-law: "She's purging off the Honeychurch taint—most excellent Honeychurches, but you know what I mean. She's not always quoting servants or asking one how the pudding's made. Cecil, mind you marry her next January! . . . Make her one of us!" Whereupon Cecil dreams out loud how his children will be educated—first in the English countryside, for freshness; then Italy, for subtlety; and then, only then, will he bring them to London.

But, before he can contemplate children, let alone their education, he must learn to kiss a girl without fretting about his pince-nez. And before he can learn that—if he ever will—the truth dawns on Lucy. One evening, in the candlelit hall at Windy Corner, she tells Cecil that their engagement must end. He is in the slightly undignified position of having just removed his shoes to climb on a chair to examine an oil painting. Dignified or not, however, he accepts his fate, and they shake hands like good fellows. Cecil, for whom our sympathy begins to stir, sits thoughtfully at the foot of the stairs and pulls on his shoes. The shot is held. What passes through his mind? We shall never know, for there he must be abandoned. After some agonized lying, Lucy admits the truth, to fatherly Mr. Emerson, and then follows her heart. At the end of *A Room with a View*, we leave her—framed against the Duomo and the Palazzo della Signoria, at an open upstairs window of the Pensione Bertolini—startled but excited, on the edge of something new and better, being covered in kisses by the eager George Emerson.

Cecil is an English snob, fastidious and foolish, but he is not a hypocrite. Merchant Ivory's next film, *Maurice* (1987), adapted from E. M. Forster's posthumous novel by Kit Hesketh-Harvey and James Ivory, dealt English sexual hypocrisy a sharp blow on the nose. The tone was serious; perhaps no other Merchant Ivory film has been more serious. Yet, the glancing comic touch, the hallmark of all Ruth Jhabvala's scripts, was not entirely absent.

The film starts with a schoolmaster, Mr. Ducie (Simon Callow), striding down the dunes towards the gusting English Channel at Rye in Sussex. He is leading an outing. Small boys vie to hold his hands. Maurice Hall is about to go to his public school, and Mr. Ducie feels he must say something about "the sacred mystery of sex," about the "membrum wirrilis" and the "waggeena." On the sand, the master draws a diagram with his walking stick.

There! Everything is clear, and need never be spoken of again. But Maurice has other ideas. "I think

THE CAFÉ ROYAL IN REGENT STREET, LONDON. CLIVE (HUGH GRANT) ENTERTAINS HIS FAMILY AND FRIENDS BEFORE SETTING OUT FOR GREECE. THE SUMPTUOUSLY PAINTED DINING ROOM DATES FROM THE 1860S.

I shan't marry," he declares, with the certainty of a twelve-year-old. Mr. Ducie has never heard such poppycock, and invites Maurice—and his wife—to dine with him and his wife ten years hence. Maurice is delighted. They have now resumed their stroll. Coming into view over the dunes, like Cecil and the ladies advancing on the Sacred Lake, is a respectable family group. Mr. Ducie turns in panic. "Those infernal diagrams!" But, Maurice reassures him, the tide will have washed them away. Lucy and her mother smiled at the cowering naked (but splendidly virile) Mr. Beebe; here, however, the parents, on their brisk seaside walk, react with dismay when their daughter stops to puzzle over Mr. Ducie's crude anatomical outlines scratched in the sand.

E. M. Forster began *Maurice* in 1913. But its significance, Ivory said, shortly before production of the film began, was its contemporary accuracy. Young men in 1986 faced the same psychological turmoil, if not the same retribution, as their forebears at the end of the Edwardian era, over which, in matters of sexual conduct, the shadow of Oscar Wilde's imprisonment, less than twenty years before, still fell. Maurice (James Wilby) in the end acknowledges his homosexuality, and with the help of a gamekeeper, Alec Scudder (Rupert Graves), finds the courage to stop living a lie. On the other hand, Clive Durham (Hugh Grant), who set Maurice on the path to self-discovery when they were both up at Cambridge in 1909, cannot bring himself to follow his friend. For fear of disgrace by association, Clive refuses to supply a character reference when another friend, Viscount Risley, is arrested for committing an act of gross indecency. Clive Durham's reward for his cowardice is respectability, a loveless marriage, and, most probably, a seat in the House of Commons.

⁂ ⁂ ⁂

AFTER CAMBRIDGE, the chief location used in *Maurice*—for Pendersleigh Park, the home of Clive, his widowed mother, and his grown-up sister—was Wilbury Park, Newton Toney, near Salisbury in Wiltshire. "We went to a grand party given at Wilton in 1978 to introduce Henry Herbert's first son," Ivory said. "Prince Charles had been invited and, since he and all his dependants were staying at Wilton, we were put up at Wilbury—that was the particular dormitory we were put in. A fellow guest was Lord Rothermere, owner of the *Daily Mail*, and the famous

Clive, upper left, delivers the Latin grace in the dining hall at King's College, Cambridge. The High Table, with its assorted Deans, Dons, and Fellows, stretches across the top.

King's College Chapel: "When the sun shines the whole vast chapel fills with colour like the inside of a casket of jewels." The cameraman, Pierre Lhomme, added his lights to the effect created by Nature and the gifted builders, in order to bring up the details of the superb fan vaulting.

LEFT: PREPARING TO FILM THE CONFIDENT UNDERGRADUATES IN THE SCENE BELOW. "THIS WAS A LITTLE SHOT," IVORY SAID, "INVOLVING A GROUP OF STUDENTS WALKING TOWARDS THE CAMERA, AS MAURICE (JAMES WILBY) WALKS BY DELIBERATELY IGNORED. BUT FEW SHOTS IN A FILM ARE TRULY *LITTLE*. THIS ONE INVOLVED LAYING A LONGISH TRACK SO THAT THE CAMERA COULD MOVE BACKWARDS AS THE PARTY ADVANCED. NORMAL UNIVERSITY TRAFFIC WAS DISRUPTED FOR THE BEST PART OF A MORNING. BY 1986, WHEN THIS SHOT WAS TAKEN, CAMBRIDGE STUDENTS WERE NO LONGER OBLIGED TO WEAR GOWNS AND MORTARBOARDS IN THE STREET."

BELOW: CONFIDENT UNDERGRADUATES, CAMBRIDGE, 1909.

LEFT: THE GOTHIC WILLIAM IV PORTER'S LODGE AT KING'S COLLEGE, CAMBRIDGE, ON A MISTY EVENING, 1909. "A FEW TELEVISION ANTENNAS CAN BE MADE OUT ABOVE THE ROOFTOPS BEYOND," IVORY SAID, "BUT THE SHOT WAS NOT HELD SO LONG THAT THE SPECTATOR'S EYE HAD TIME TO WANDER."

Maria St. Just (Maria Britneva) in the character of Mrs. Sheepshanks.

'Bubbles,' I remember, made an entrance. I had no idea who she was—I thought perhaps she might be a maid. [Viscount Rothermere's wife was an effervescent socialite with an emphatic dress sense.] Peter Shaffer, author of *Amadeus*, was also among our party. After that, I became quite friendly with Maria St. Just, the owner of Wilbury Park. She took to me, I guess." A friend of Tennessee Williams, Lady St. Just became the playwright's literary executor, and the editor (with Kit Hesketh-Harvey) of a selection of his letters. She had acted at one time under the name Maria Britneva, and she later prevailed on Ivory to give her the part of the overbearing Mrs. Vyse in *A Room with a View*—for which, Ivory said, she was ideal.

"By 1978, however, we had only got as far as *The Europeans*, which was enjoying great success in England [it was then the longest-running film at London's Curzon cinema] In fact, Ismail asked Prince Charles whether he'd seen it. He said, 'No.' And Ismail said, 'Why? You must see it. . . .' When we first stayed at Wilbury Park, I was given a room called the 'Red Room,' which was so long and narrow, and so full of mahogany furniture, it was a bit like being in a Victorian wagon-lit. The house was called the first Palladian house in England, but people don't really give that much credit. Over time, it was enlarged, and wings were added. Wilbury came into the possession of Maria's father-in-law, Lord St. Just, about 1920. He was J. P. Morgan's English partner, and together they founded Morgan Grenfell Bank, so there was a certain amount of money there."

Katya Grenfell, one of Lady St. Just's two daughters, acted as a stills photographer on *A Room with a View* and *Maurice*. And Maria herself was cast in *Maurice* as "Woolly," Mrs. Durham's trying friend Mrs. Sheepshanks. Lady St. Just's two large dogs also appear in the film. Hopeful of a titbit, they poke their noses up from under the table during a smart formal dinner. And after a suitable, very English pause their mistress rewards them with an endearment and a broken biscuit. In another scene, lolloping on a landing, the dogs look, quite correctly, as if they own the house. "Maria was terribly good in the scene when Mrs. Sheepshanks climbs down from the carriage and Mrs. Durham [Judy Parfitt] comes out and they have some talk. That accent, that attitude—hair-raising! But Maria, who died in 1994, wasn't in fact English, she was Russian, one hundred percent Russian."

The boathouse where Maurice first breaks, and finally keeps, his tryst with Alec Scudder was in the grounds of a house named Crichel, in Dorset. "It was a mid-eighteenth-century grey block of a house with many arresting features," Ivory said. "There was an immense stairwell which went up four floors. It was square, and on the walls were

A Bermondsey gym: Maurice (James Wilby) gives a boxing lesson. E. M. Forster performed similar good works among the underprivileged of London's East End.

Alec Scudder (Rupert Graves) at the crease.

Simcox the butler (Patrick Godfrey) and the ladder to Maurice's bedroom.

huge paintings in grisaille. There was no other colour in the hall. The stairs themselves were, I think, a kind of scrubbed oak. They were as clean as a butcher board. You made a wonderful clomping sound going up the stairs, and they looked equally wonderful. Unfortunately, the lake was very mucky. But there was a proper boathouse—you see a little of it in daylight when Scudder, the gamekeeper who climbs through Maurice's bedroom window, is writing the letter to Maurice in the rain—a pseudo-Gothic 'cottage' circa 1890."

MAURICE (JAMES WILBY) AND ALEC SCUDDER (RUPERT GRAVES).

For his second Forster film, Ivory went back to one of his favourite London locations, the Linley Sambourne House, in Stafford Terrace, Kensington (see p. 51). "After the cartoonist Linley Sambourne's death, the house passed to one of his descendants, the Countess of Rosse, grandmother of the photographer Lord Snowdon. The Linley Sambourne House is not unlike the equally well preserved Gibson House, on Beacon Street, Boston, which we used in 1983 for *The Bostonians.* That was of about the same period, and decorated in the corresponding American style, although it was not the home of an artist, but of business people. We used the Linley Sambourne House first for *A Room with a View,* and then returned for *Maurice,* and I'm surprised we didn't go back for *Howards End.* (We never did get to the bedrooms.) We didn't re-dress the rooms, which is rare for us; in fact we hardly touched them. We were in and out very quickly, one day for *A Room with a View,* two for *Maurice.*" The Bermondsey gym, where Maurice gives boxing lessons to the dockers, was the same building in which Forster himself did his charitable work among the East End poor. In the gym's vault (it is now a school) there are said to be many letters from Forster.

ONE OF E. M. FORSTER'S biographers, Lord Annan, wrote that Forster did not admire public schools [that is, private schools] or their products whom he described as having 'well-developed bodies, fairly developed minds and undeveloped hearts.' . . . His unhappiness [at Tonbridge School, Kent] melted and his potentialities appeared only when he went in 1897 as a classical exhibitioner to King's College, Cambridge,. where, as he wrote later, 'They taught the perky boy that he was not everything, and the limp boy that he might be something.'" Between 1927 and 1933, Forster was a fellow of King's; and in 1946, he was elected to an honorary fellowship and invited to make the college his home.

All the Cambridge interiors for *Maurice* were set in King's College; and in fact, the undergraduate room

Alec Scudder (Rupert Graves) waits for Maurice in the boathouse at Pendersleigh Park.

Left: Punting on the Backs at Cambridge: Maurice, Clive Durham, and their aristocratic friend Risley. Clare College is to the right.

Maurice (James Wilby) with Scudder's parents and sharp-eyed brother aboard the sailing ship that should have taken the affectionate gamekeeper of Pendersleigh Park to the Argentine and a better life.

Wilbury Park. Cameraman Pierre Lhomme aims his camera into a carriage during an artificial downpour.

Left: Gloucester Docks.

Filming Risley's trial for indecency at the Salisbury town hall, Wiltshire.

ENGLISH JUSTICE: VISCOUNT RISLEY (MARK TANDY) IN THE DOCK.

containing the player piano, which Maurice and Clive use for Lord Risley's paper copy of the "Pathetic Symphony," has a door opening on to Forster's former quarters (now used as a faculty sitting room, and having, as Ivory said, "no real owner"). The fellows of King's were, it seems, pleased to welcome Merchant Ivory (Forster left his royalties to his alma mater), and the only minor squall the crew ran into while dealing with the authorities was over the use of King's College Chapel, where precedence and ancient procedure were not, it seems, on one occasion adhered to, and what was to have been a grand candlelit scene inside one of England's greatest rooms was reduced to two brief shots, of a stall of choristers, and a hurriedly departing Maurice.

King's traditional rival, Trinity College, was used for a few exterior shots, in the quadrangle, opposite and under the Wren Library, and at the college gates and porter's lodge. "There was not really, in our experience, a sense of rivalry between the two ancient colleges," Ivory said, "more a sense of foolishness. Nevertheless, Ismail did have to recruit a very high-powered Indian girl, a friend of his, to whip up the fellows at Trinity. They were rallied to force the bursar to accept us, and he did accept. That said, when we were shooting in the Trinity quadrangle, some old man—I don't know who he was—appeared in a fury and tried to put his hand in front of the camera. The crew didn't exactly manhandle him, but they did take him away."

⁂ ⁂ ⁂

THE HYPOCRITES lie as thick upon the ground in *Maurice* as autumn leaves. When Maurice is sent down from Cambridge, for cutting lectures and, on one occasion, roaring off on his motorcycle with Durham in the passenger seat under the nose of the infuriated Dean Cornwallis (Barry Foster), he has a manly talk with his mother's friend Dr. Barry (Denholm Elliott). Their conversation, beginning amicably if a little delicately, turns abruptly vicious as Dr. Barry rounds on Maurice for the hurt he is causing his mother by refusing to write a letter of apology to the Dean. Dr. Barry, who later examines Maurice for the expected symptoms of venereal disease, with a distasteful matter-of-factness, is not unlike a Cambridge official who had attempted to thwart the shoot of *Maurice*. "This man had a pale face," Ivory said, "with lanky hair over a skull-like brow. And as Ismail took him to one side, I really thought he was not human. This was the kind of man who voted for the execution of Charles I—not that he didn't deserve to have his head cut off, maybe he did—maddened and inflexible, and very English."

Another marvellously vivid hypocrite, though one forced into hypocrisy, at least partly, by the nature of his job, is Simcox, the West Country butler of Pendersleigh Park. He is played by Patrick Godfrey—the peevish Dr.

Clive Durham (Hugh Grant).

Saunders of *Heat and Dust*, driven to distracted fury by the lying habits of the Indians; and the complacent Mr. Eager of *A Room with a View*, who on the outing to Fiesole senses impropriety and orders off the driver's seat the over-familiar coachman's beautiful companion—and he shows by everything he says and does that he knows exactly what is going on between the young master (who of course does nothing to moderate his behaviour in front of the servants) and his uncertain Cambridge friend. Simcox glances at Maurice and Durham with a look of that particular insolent disdain—which English servants reserve for their employers—as he bicycles past them down a country path, his long dark coat and bowler hat an exact complement to his bottled-up propriety. He sees the mud from Scudder's boots on Maurice's bedroom carpet, and observes coldly that it will need cleaning up. Simcox has a repellent fascination: he is emphatically not from the Hollywood school of English butlering Ivory had encountered in the films of his youth.

Against these hypocrites—and there are more: Lasker Jones, the quack hypnotist; Dean Cornwallis himself, grown weary of all the too-clever young men who have passed through his tutorial room; the Reverend Mr. Borenius, a skull-faced cleric, anxious to see Scudder confirmed before he departs for the perils of the Argentine—is pitted the human and essentially normal Maurice, a large, friendly, middle-class Englishman, whose undeveloped sense of ambition is what perhaps allows him to see life whole and to embark, at the end of the film, on the defiantly happy road that Forster lays down for him. The closing moment of the film has Clive gazing out of his bedroom window, as Simcox makes his rounds securing the shutters against the night.

NIGHT FALLS: CLIVE DURHAM (HUGH GRANT) AND HIS WIFE, ANNE (PHOEBE NICHOLLS).

GAZETTEER

The opening scenes of *Maurice*, set in Cambridge between Michaelmas 1909 and Summer 1910, were shot chiefly at **King's College**, which received its charter in 1441, and whose grandeur, said one writer, absorbs the imagination. The chief glory of **King's College Chapel**, which was begun in 1446 and completed by Henry VIII, is its stained-glass windows. "When the sun shines the whole vast chapel fills with colour like the inside of a casket of jewels." The punting scene, in which Maurice is mocked, was taken on the **River Cam** at **Clare Bridge**; and outside college views of **Trinity**, **Clare**, and **Caius** are also featured.

The field in which Maurice and Clive have their one moment of (almost) unclouded happiness, after speeding away from Dean Cornwallis, was situated near **Ely** in Cambridgeshire. Durham's country home, Pendersleigh, was the private house of Lady St. Just, **Wilbury Park**, near Newton Toney, on the A338, in Wiltshire; and the **Town Hall** at **Salisbury**, Wiltshire, served as both Maurice's London office (where he studies the ticker tape) and the court where Viscount Risley is sentenced to jail with hard labour after his entrapment by a cherry-coated guardsman. The Art Nouveau tavern in which Risley tries to pick up the soldier is in reality the **Blackfriar**, formerly part of a thirteenth-century Dominican Priory, at 174 Queen Victoria Street, London EC4.

The ground-floor dining room of the **Café Royal**, Regent Street, London W1, was the setting for Durham's farewell party for family and friends, while the Grecian amphitheatre where Durham retires to collect his thoughts was the ruin at **Segesta**, near Castellammare, in northwest Sicily. Ten years after the scene on the beach at **Rye**, in Sussex, Mr. Ducie and his wife encounter Maurice and Scudder in the **Assyrian Saloon** of the **British Museum**, Great Russell Street, London WC1. Mr. Ducie cannot remember Maurice's name; and Maurice is no doubt relieved to escape the promised invitation to dinner. The room in which Maurice and Alec subsequently make love was in the office of an arts establishment in **Bedford Square**, Bloomsbury, near the British Museum; and the sailing ship aboard which Scudder had planned to go to the Argentine to start a new life was moored at **Gloucester** docks on the **River Severn**.

Cambridge contains thirty-one university colleges, the chapels, quadrangles, and certain gardens of which are open to visitors on most days (Tel. 01223 322640). **King's College Chapel**; the **Pepys Library**, at the diarist's old college, Magdalene; the **Fitzwilliam Museum** (open all year, certain days, Tel. 01223 332900); and the **University Botanic Garden** (open all year, daily, Tel. 01223 336265) are among the city's delights. Those desiring a view should climb the tower of **Great Saint Mary's Church** (open all year, daily, Tel. 01223 350914).

Wimpole Hall: off the A14, 8 miles southwest of Cambridge, open April to late October, certain days, Tel. 01223 207257. A place of pilgrimage for bibliophiles: here, Lord Harley assembled the books and prints known as the Harleian Miscellany, which became the heart of the British Library. Begun in the 1640s and much restored by its last private owner, Rudyard Kipling's daughter, Mrs. Elsie Bambridge, the house contains a splendid yellow drawing room designed by Sir John Soane.

Wilton House: off the A30 at Wilton, west of Salisbury, open April to October, daily, Tel. 01722 743115.

James Ivory believed, with justice, that Wilton, the sixteenth-century home of his friend Henry Herbert, the Earl of Pembroke, was simply too grand a building for "Darlington Hall," the chief set of *The Remains of the Day*. Here is the famous Palladian Bridge (and within the house Inigo Jones' single and double cube rooms) of a million post-cards. At Wilton, it is said, Shakespeare gave the first performance of *Twelfth Night*.

Salisbury Cathedral: Salisbury, open all year, daily, Tel. 01722 335659. *The* great subject of landscape painters, especially Constable, the cathedral, begun in 1220, completed 1258, has the tallest and most elegant spire in England, and is noted for its Early English pointed arches and its exceptionally tall windows.

Stonehenge: off the A303, 2 miles west of Amesbury, open all year, daily, Tel. 0117 973 4472. Once seen, this unique, mysterious, prehistoric configuration of mighty stones on a ridge of Salisbury Plain is never forgotten. Be prepared for crowds of fellow visitors.

Longleat House: off the A362, 4 miles southeast of Frome, open all year, daily, Tel. 0198 584 4400. Four years after World War II, the Marquis of Bath became the first English landowner to open his house to the public on a commercial basis. He also opened, in 1966, Britain's first safari park (the "Lions of Longleat"), furiously opposed at the time, but now a cornerstone of the leisure industry. The immense house, decorated in the Italian Renaissance style, is the height of gilded magnificence. Do not miss the Great Hall (containing the shirt of lace Charles I was wearing when executed), the Red Library, and the three dining rooms, set for breakfast, lunch, and dinner.

"The ghost of Longleat is that of the second Viscountess Weymouth," wrote a contributor to a *Sunday Times* travel guide more than forty years ago. "Her portrait painted in a pastoral masquerade-dress, hangs in one of the downstairs rooms, and she has a gay, sly, wilful face, with great good looks. Her husband's portrait hangs there too—he is silly, heavy and plain. Early in her married life the Viscountess introduced her lover, disguised as a footman, into Longleat. After eleven years the dull-witted Viscount penetrated the disguise, killed the lover, and buried him secretly at night under a flagstone in one of the cellars. The lady died of grief and searches the houses for her lost lover. Twenty years ago they took up the cellar flags for some reason, and found the body; it crumbled into dust at the touch of the air, in the approved fashion. It is exactly like an Ingoldsby legend from first to last: love, betrayal, murder, cellars, flagstones and crumblings—all quite complete."

Tourist Information Centres/Accommodation: Wheeler Street, Cambridge CB2 3QB; Tel. 01223 322640/ Fax 01223 463385. Fish Row, Salisbury, Wiltshire SP1 1EJ; Tel. 01722 334956/Fax 01722 422059.
Travel London–Cambridge: Trains from King's Cross and Liverpool Street stations. By car, M25, M11.
London–Salisbury: Trains from Waterloo station. By car, M25, M3, A30.

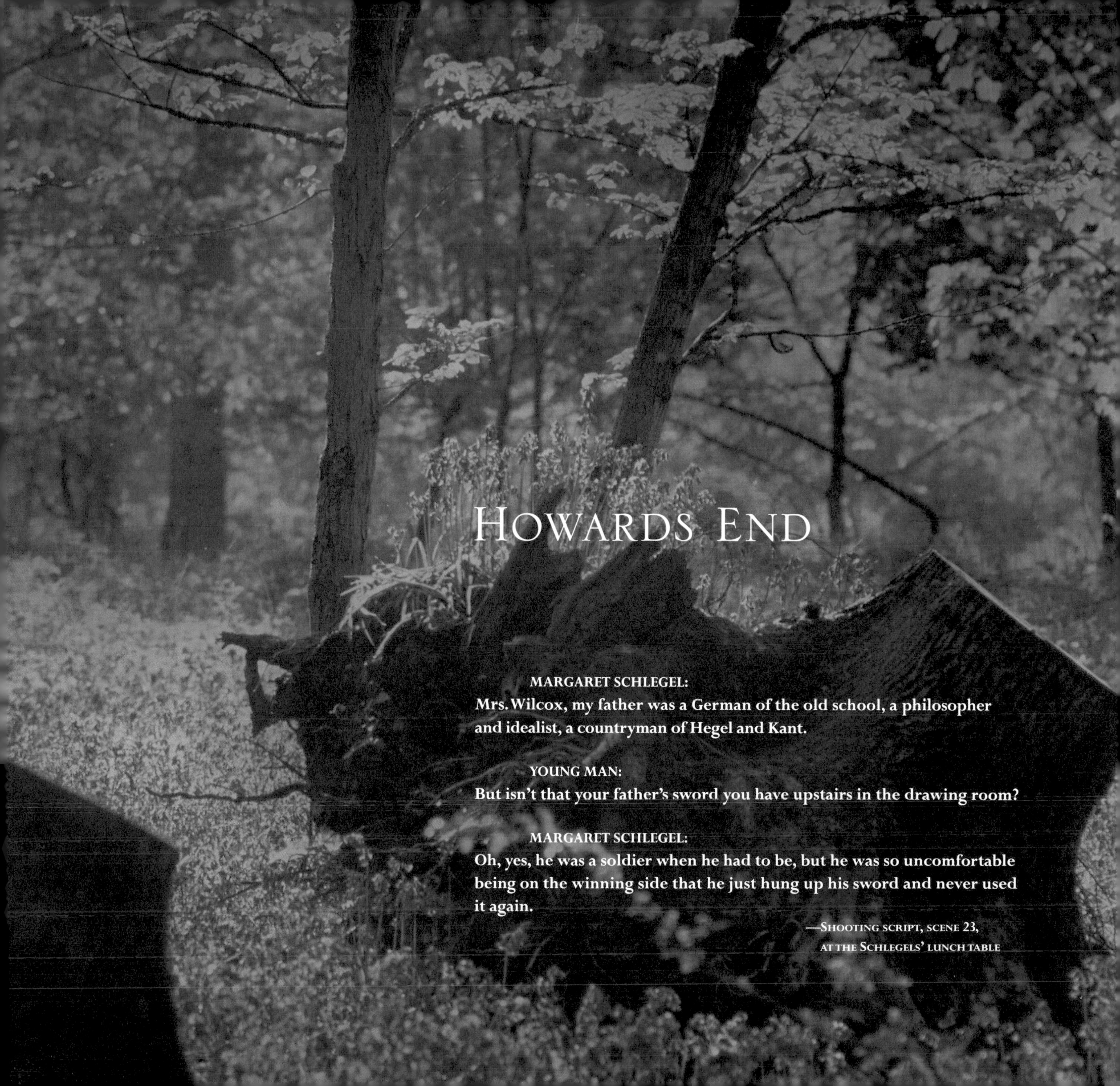

Howards End

MARGARET SCHLEGEL:
Mrs. Wilcox, my father was a German of the old school, a philosopher and idealist, a countryman of Hegel and Kant.

YOUNG MAN:
But isn't that your father's sword you have upstairs in the drawing room?

MARGARET SCHLEGEL:
Oh, yes, he was a soldier when he had to be, but he was so uncomfortable being on the winning side that he just hung up his sword and never used it again.

—Shooting script, scene 23,
at the Schlegels' lunch table

The Schlegel sisters, Meg (Emma Thompson) and Helen (Helena Bonham Carter).

Pages 74–75: Leonard Bast (Samuel West) amid the bluebells.

THE ANGLO-GERMAN SISTERS at the centre of *Howards End* will have nothing to do with hypocrisy. Like Maurice Hall and Lucy Honeychurch, Margaret and Helen Schlegel (Emma Thompson and Helena Bonham Carter) have lost their father—and, worse, their English mother too. They have no Mrs. Hall, and no surrogate mother such as Mrs. Durham, no Mrs. Honeychurch or anxious Miss Charlotte Bartlett, no honorary sisters or siblings who look up to them, only a worrisome aunt (Prunella Scales) and a limp brother (Adrian Ross Magenty), on whom they dote like the overindulgent parents they never had.

They must look out for themselves, give instructions to the maid, play hostess to the new neighbours, dispense calling cards. They must find a new home when the lease on their present one expires. (They have lived since birth in their parents' comfortable, well-furnished West London house, and they are fussy, so the task is not going to be easy.) Their hair, especially Helen's, seems not to wish to have anything to do with pins. They run up and down stairs; they are purposeful; they do not pick at their food. They pay attention in the company of original people—or ordinary people, like the clerk Leonard Bast (Samuel West), who do extraordinary things, such as taking a walk in the country in the middle of the night using the polestar for a compass. Above all, they talk and talk. Nothing will stop them rattling on; and they have the habit, before they can stop themselves, of speaking the truth, as they see it. They are exhausting, memorable, and slightly larger than life.

Howards End is the most ambitious of Merchant Ivory's three Forster adaptations. Unlike *A Room with a View*, a comedy of manners, and *Maurice*, a story somewhat burdened, some have found, by the weight of its confessional tone, *Howards End* was drawn from a magisterial, full-rigged English novel sailing under the bright colours of E. M. Forster's particular brand of compassionate English humanism. Its theme, put briefly, is the defeat of hypocrisy through a combination of truth-telling and the workings of mystical good fortune, with the result that the wish of the dying Mrs. Wilcox—that her house, Howards End, be passed to the homeless Margaret Schlegel—is satisfactorily fulfilled, if not in quite the way Mrs. Wilcox imagined. Howards End stands, in a sense, for everything that is settled and honourable about England.

⁂

HOWARDS END, the film, unfolds across a broad canvas. As the curtain parts, the names of the five Japanese backers come edging in from the left of the screen, like a fleet of war canoes, and then, with the music rising to a climax, a painting of three vivid dancers dissolves in from the black. "I saw a reproduction of André Derain's *La Danse*," James Ivory said, "in a copy of the American Express *Departures* magazine, featuring a big Fauve show at the Tate Gallery. 'How can I use this,' I asked myself—I had a similar thought when I saw the 'Mud People' of *Savages* in a magazine advertisement all those years ago. The date of the painting was 1906, and because it was the advanced art of its day, I imagined Margaret and Helen might just possibly have gone to an exhibition and seen it.

"Then I did some research and found that Derain had painted many many pictures of London—Regent Street, Hyde Park, all along the Thames, the various train stations—and I had the idea of incorporating some of these into the film. But then we calculated the cost . . . and used only *La Danse*. The Schlegels were always talking about advanced art in the book. But perhaps the Fauves would have been a bit too advanced. I don't know. Their work was not that different from the work of some contemporary English artists. The Fauves were wilder and more exuberant, but the way they broke down the forms into areas of colour wasn't that removed from what was then being done in England."

RUTH WILCOX (VANESSA REDGRAVE), AT LUNCH WITH THE SCHLEGELS AND THEIR TALKATIVE FRIENDS.

Something of the Fauve spirit animates the Schlegel sisters. They have a broad outlook, they have experienced more than just England. Ranged against them, however, is an English clan, the Wilcoxes, who never dream of lifting their eyes to the sky. Henry Wilcox (Anthony Hopkins), the paterfamilias, is the worst. Burdened with an invalid wife, a suspicious daughter, and two unpromising sons, he is both a bully and a hypocrite. He is a man who doubtless bought books by the yard; and he certainly bought a house complete with all its ancestral oil paintings. He knows what's what, and appears to trust no one but himself. He has made a heap of money from a West African rubber company. One scene in particular sums him up.

Mr. Wilcox is courting his neighbour Margaret Schlegel, whom he first met on holiday in Germany, and he has contrived a meeting at Simpson's-in-the-Strand, the restaurant famous for its traditional English fare. He has secured a table—always prudent to secure a table. Mr. Wilcox is not a man to leave anything to chance. He seats everyone, like a superior usher, overrides Margaret's choice of fish pie, scans the menu without reading it, and orders roast beef and Yorkshire pudding (the meat well-done for himself), and cider to drink. He gives the menu a little flick with his fingers, a gesture of both dismissal and exuberance. He ostentatiously tips the carver and then—assuming the servants

Ruth Wilcox, the owner of Howards End, observes her family and their guest Helen Schlegel.

Christmas shopping at Fortnum & Mason.

are deaf—announces that he believes in tipping everywhere. Tipping, he declares, is especially efficacious in the East, "a few piasters properly distributed keeps the memory green." How cynical, Margaret retorts. Not a bit of it, he says, simply realistic.

Henry's son Charles is a shadow of his father, but without the authority. He clamps down on his pipe as if to give himself strength. His eyes bulge with mute anger. His clothes are too tight, his collar cuts into his neck. Everything about him seems repressed and unhappy. His wife's voice is a squeaky whine. She never says the right thing, which irritates Charles, but he knows he must be polite to her, which adds to his frustration. The Schlegels are anathema to him, he distrusts their "artistic beastliness." They stand for everything uncertain and unsettled. They must have their arguments. He is the sort of man who calls his father *Sir* in a moment of crisis, not because he respects his father—he probably fears him—but because he believes it is what will please the old dictator. James Wilby—the hero of *Maurice*—plays the philistine Charles Wilcox. What punishment, one wonders, would Henry Wilcox have inflicted on this simpleton had he not turned out a red-blooded, heterosexual facsimile of his hard-hearted father?

MEG (EMMA THOMPSON) PAYS A LAST VISIT TO RUTH WILCOX (VANESSA REDGRAVE), WHOSE DYING WISH—LATER SCRIBBLED ON A SCRAP OF PAPER—WAS THAT HOWARDS END BE GIVEN TO HER HOMELESS FRIEND AND SPIRITUAL HEIR.

PAGES 82–83. HONITON, THE SCENE OF THE BLIGHTED WEDDING RECEPTION. THE LOCATION WAS BRAMPTON BRYAN, HEREFORD AND WORCESTER.

Leonard Bast (Samuel West) in pursuit of his stolen umbrella.

⁂ ⁂ ⁂

WE DO NOT SEE Helen Schlegel touring any exhibition—or standing before a Renaissance painting in the National Gallery (like Cecil in *A Room with a View*) or an Assyrian monolith at the British Museum (like Mr. Ducie in *Maurice*); she does, however, attend a lecture on "Music and Meaning" at the Ethical Hall. A Scottish speaker (Simon Callow) is holding forth on the images suggested by Beethoven's Fifth Symphony. Goblin footsteps, he asserts, can be heard in the third movement. The pianist demonstrates. "Why—*specifically*—goblin?" asks a forceful, long-haired gentleman in the audience. He is the scriptwriter Ruth Jhabvala's brother, Siegbert Prawer, Emeritus Professor of German at Oxford University, and author of, among books on English, German, and comparative literature, *Caligari's Children*, subtitled "The Film as Tale of Terror." Before the speaker can answer, however, the camera leaves him: Helen has swept up the umbrella hanging from the seat in front of her, and exited into the rain, pursued by the umbrella's owner, the distinctly clodhopping Leonard Bast.

AT WICKHAM PLACE: LEONARD BAST ALARMED BY THE UNEXPECTED GENEROSITY OF THE SCHLEGELS.

Leonard longs for something new and better. Clerking at the Porphyrion insurance company is dull. He balances a dip pen on his nose, smiles like a guilty child at his unseen neighbour, and then, instead of checking figures, applies himself to an atlas of the heavens. At home, his friend Jacky, a large, cheerful girl, would rather have him in bed than sitting beside the fire marking important passages in uplifting books. He tends to be querulous in her company. The role of householder, at least in that dispiriting house, does not appeal to him, and probably never will.

When Helen spots Leonard lingering in the street, a sodden newspaper over his bowler hat, he is invited indoors and rushed upstairs on a wave of Schlegel hospitality. Helen whisks a plate of scones from her brother, Tibby, who is preparing to wolf the lot. Margaret hastily pours a cup of China tea. Plate and teacup are thrust at Leonard: he is overwhelmed, the gap between them yawns. All this generosity, intelligence—money! Even if he accepts their tea, he sees, he knows, what he can never have, however many times he goes to the Ethical Hall, or however many times he reads his John Ruskin and his Walter Pater. Back in his garret, with Margaret Schlegel's card as his bookmark, he refuses the meal Jacky has left out for him. A half-eaten cottage loaf sits on the table; and Jacky, not liking to see food go to waste, picks up Leonard's slice of cold meat with her fingers and drops it in her mouth.

JACKY (NICOLA DUFFETT) WANTS THE TRUTH ABOUT HER FIANCÉ, LEONARD BAST, AND HIS FRIEND MARGARET SCHLEGEL.

"Say it was all about Leonard Bast," Ruth Jhabvala said. "Imagine if this 'England' of Merchant Ivory's films was all about Leonard Bast!" But do there not have to be Leonard Basts? "No, not really, he was the only one—and he was an embarrassment. I mean to have to reconstruct his dingy quarters! He was as much an embarrassment to them [Merchant and Ivory] as he was to E. M. Forster, who also didn't like to descend into that milieu."

How does Ivory answer the charge? "Ruth is speaking humorously—unfortunately, she's also providing our critics (mostly American), who say we are so elitist, with more ammunition. But I don't agree with her about Forster's 'embarrassment' at descending into the Basts' milieu. All his life, Forster tried to do this, to break through class and colour barriers—sometimes too self-consciously, or out of idealism, when it didn't work; and sometimes romantically, when it did, as with the trolley-car ticket taker, Mohammed el Adl, or the policeman, Bob Buckingham. I imagine Forster's eye and ear for the details of working-class life—speech, living arrangements, dress, and of course his sensitive shadings of class behaviour—were as acute as when registering the behaviour of the upper classes.

"On the other hand, Ruth is right when she implies that I'd soon grow tired of spending too much time reconstructing the world of Leonard Bast. But then that's also true of America. What if I had to spend my life reconstructing the lives of the kind of conventional American families found on TV and in most Hollywood movies? A 'real' American family, an American version of the Basts—well, my heart sinks.

HENRY WILCOX (ANTHONY HOPKINS) AFTER PROPOSING MARRIAGE TO MEG.

"But I did enjoy doing Leonard's home life, to an extent, but not as much as doing the Schlegels' home life, that was more fun. It was interesting to show Clive Durham's world in *Maurice*; and very interesting to show Lord Darlington's world in *The Remains of the Day*. But what if I had to make films just about those kind of people? It would be equally dull. I do best with educated upper-middle-class people like myself. The people of *The Householder* were of the genteel-poor middle class. I was inspired at that point by those kinds of people in Satyajit Ray movies. Ray had taken young couples like that, again and again. People aspiring to a better life, and forced to live in some miserable room. And never for a second is it ever dull. That's what kept me going on Prem and Indu from *The Householder*. But basically, I feel better off with people who are reasonably articulate. When you know something about what they are thinking, and why, they're not foreign to one.

"If you think about the films Ismail has directed, all his films right the balance in Merchant Ivory. Because if we are interested in lords and movie stars and the kinds of people we make films about, he has only shown in his films—*Mahatma and the Mad Boy* [1972] and *The Courtesans of Bombay* [1983]—the lives of very poor people, people who struggle. His new film, *In Custody* [1993], is the whole world of the Indian *ustad* artists, who don't have any money, most of them, unless they are famous recording stars. There will be poor people in our next film,

Mr. Wilcox orders lunch for four at Simpson's-in-the-Strand.

THORNTON'S
Steam Laundry
PADDINGTON

Above: The coronation procession of Queen Elizabeth II, on its way to Westminster Abbey, June 2, 1953, as it passes through Admiralty Arch.

Left: Admiralty Arch, which takes its name from its proximity to the Admiralty, headquarters of the Royal Navy, was erected in 1911 by Edward VII in memory of his mother, Queen Victoria. "One might call it London's Triumphal Arch," Ivory said. "Unlike that of Paris, however, traffic runs through it in both directions. Admiralty Arch is linked forever with Britain's grandest public spectacles, and was the only such monument that we, as filmmakers, could isolate from modern London to re-create a semblance of the turn-of-the-century city."

MEG (EMMA THOMPSON) SOFTENS UP HER FUTURE HUSBAND (ANTHONY HOPKINS), WHOM SHE HOPES WILL GIVE A JOB TO HER SISTER'S OUT-OF-WORK PROTÉGÉ, LEONARD BAST.

Jefferson in Paris, slaves and the aggrieved French populace. I don't quite know how I shall get myself into the way of thinking about what it was like to be a slave. What was it like actually to *be* a slave? To belong to someone who could sell you, or impregnate you with the intention of breeding future slaves? And it's equally difficult to get into the mind of the slave owner who would do such things."

⁂ ⁂ ⁂

MERCHANT IVORY'S England does not scorn the obvious. Margaret Schlegel goes with Mrs. Wilcox (Vanessa Redgrave) on a Christmas shopping trip to Fortnum & Mason, the Piccadilly food store renowned for the rarity and profusion of its goods, and its swallow-tailed gentleman attendants. And on the way there, she passes under Admiralty Arch, the immense triumphal gate leading from The Mall to Trafalgar Square—though she does not, like her fellow chatterbox Nirad Chaudhuri in *Adventures of a Brown Man*, take several turns round the square itself. Steam trains and polished vintage cars are made much of; groomed horses, drays and carriages, all add to the texture of this imagined England.

But also preserved and recorded are the less obvious. James Ivory, the collector, once observed that one motive for his buying Indian paintings was sometimes to preserve them from white ants and dust, and the depredations of the Indian climate. Tucked away in all Merchant Ivory's films are small acts of architectural and artistic conservation:

an expanding view of the Piazza della Signoria in Florence; a collage of Italian statuary; details of staircases and stained-glass windows; a brief angled shot of the doorway of a prosperous Harley Street building; the facade of Howards End—a red-brick "cottage" covered in wisteria blossoms.

"My production designer Luciana Arrighi knew Roger and Caroline Shapland, the owners of Peppard Cottage, which became our Howards End," Ivory said. "The house was seven or eight miles from Henley and looked amazingly like Rooksnest, Forster's home in Stevenage. Rooksnest was slightly taller and slightly more flat-fronted, but it was basically the same—a long house, with dormer windows and a porch, like the little peaked porch that sticks out in the film. Peppard Cottage, which I believe began as a small rudimentary farmhouse in the seventeenth century, was formerly owned by Lady Ottoline Morrell, the influential literary hostess [1873–1938], who remodelled it a lot and added bay windows. There was a skylight in one of the bedrooms through which Ottoline was said to have lowered her boyfriends.

"Forster described Howards End as having a great wych elm, but we had to have a horse chestnut for the tree in which the pigs' teeth are embedded—all the elms on Peppard Common having been destroyed by Dutch elm disease years ago. We got on extremely well with the Shaplands; there were many many rooms, which helps, and we were in the front, while they went on living in the back. People whose houses we've used are, I've found, much easier to deal with on a long-term basis. Endless trouble comes out of two days. But when there's an invasion and occupation, people seem to get on better and become interested."

Henry Wilcox with Margaret Schlegel and her Aunt Juley on a lawn above the sweep of Blackpool Sands, Devon. In the foreground, Helen Schlegel watches in helpless misery (left to right: Helena Bonham Carter, Anthony Hopkins, Emma Thompson, Prunella Scales).

Howards End: Charles (James Wilby), Evie (Jemma Redgrave), Mrs. Wilcox (Vanessa Redgrave), and Paul (Joseph Bennett), the younger brother who started all the trouble with Helen Schlegel. The house, Peppard Cottage near Henley-on-Thames, resembled E. M. Forster's childhood home, Rooksnest, and, like it, had medieval origins poking crookedly out of its Victorian sheath.

Gazetteer

The Schlegel home, 6 Wickham Place, was a private house in a Regency row in **Victoria Square**, close to Buckingham Palace Gardens, Westminster. (The apartment block behind it was created by a matte effect.) The Schlegels looked across the street at the Wilcoxes from the back of their house. "But the Wilcoxes," Ivory said, "were all over the place"—at the **St. James Court Hotel**, in Buckingham Gate; and at the **Royal Holloway and Bedford New College**, London University, at Egham, Surrey. The inner college contains a series of rooms (circa 1860) noted for their stamped-leather hangings, one of which became the sitting room where Meg called on the invalid Mrs. Wilcox. The quadrangle of the college was also used for the shot of the dejected Henry Wilcox on the hospital veranda.

Oxford Town Hall doubled as the Ethical Hall, though the gates outside were situated in an alley near the **Bank of England**, in the City of London. Meg and Mrs. Wilcox buy railway tickets to Hilton, where passengers disembark for Howards End, at London's **St. Pancras Station**, on the Euston Road; Hilton station itself was at **Bewdley**, a stop on the Severn Valley Railway, in Hereford and Worcester. The interior of Leonard and Jacky's flat was re-created above **Andrew Edmunds**, the Lexington Street restaurant, on the outskirts of Soho. (The London office of Merchant Ivory Productions crams into two rooms at 46 Lexington Street.) And Leonard points to the stars while standing on the roof of a house in **Union Street**, in Southwark, near London Bridge. The establishing shot of Oxford was taken from the tower of **New College**; and the study in which Tibby Schlegel eats his apple charlotte, and is later browbeaten by Charles Wilcox, was at **Magdalen College**.

The scenes at Howards End, and in the bluebell wood, through which Leonard wanders, were taken at or near the private home **Peppard Cottage**, on Peppard Common, Oxfordshire. Mr. Wilcox proposed to Margaret on the suitably grand stairs of the office in **South Audley Street**, Mayfair, belonging to Albert "Cubby" Broccoli, the American producer of the James Bond films. The house of her Aunt Juley from which Meg is summoned to the lunch at **Simpson's-in-the-Strand** (100, The Strand, London W1) was owned by the man who in 1953 organized the coronation of Queen Elizabeth II; the building, which was haunted (and unmistakably so, according to one member of the production team), overlooked the English Channel at **Blackpool Sands**, near Dartmouth, Devon.

When Mr. Wilcox strolls with the Schlegel sisters along Chelsea Embankment, they are in fact on **Chiswick Mall**. The immense hall of the Porphyrion insurance company was filmed at the abandoned **Pearl Assurance Building**, High Holborn in the City; and the panelled rooms of Mr. Wilcox's Imperial and West African Rubber Company were created in an upstairs suite of the same building. The **Baltic Exchange**, in Saint Mary Axe, off Leadenhall Street, also in the City, was used for the banking institution where Leonard applies in vain for work. (When the Exchange was later wrecked by a bomb, planted by the Irish Republican Army, Merchant Ivory was asked for location photographs of the interior to assist in its reconstruction.)

Brampton Bryan, an eighteenth-century private house on the Welsh border, near Ludlow, was used for Honiton, Mr. Wilcox's country mansion. As seen in the film, the house has a small adjoining castle. The Harley family, formerly Earls of Oxford, have lived at Brampton Bryan for many generations; and during the Civil War, a Lady

Brilliana Harley, in the absence of her husband, successfully withstood a six-week Royalist siege. The George tavern near Honiton, to which the Basts are despatched after Jacky has disgraced herself at the Wilcox family wedding, was at **Upper Arley**, north of Bewdley; and the rowing expedition which ends with Leonard in Helen's arms took place on a nearby stretch of the **River Severn**.

As at Cambridge, the majority of the thirty-five university colleges at **Oxford** are open to the public on most afternoons (Tel. 01865 276154). In addition to **Magdalen College**, with its tranquil riverside walk named after the essayist Joseph Addison, founder of the *Spectator*, the visitor on the trail of Merchant Ivory may care to call at the **Ashmolean Museum** (open all year, certain days, Tel. 01865 278000), the home of Uccello's panoramic *Hunt in the Forest*; **Pembroke College**, **Christ Church**, and **All Souls**, where scenes from *Adventures of a Brown Man in Search of Civilization* were photographed; and **Carfax Tower**, at the city centre, which commands fine views from its summit (open March to November, daily, Tel. 01865 792653).

Blenheim Palace: off the A34 in Woodstock, open mid-March to October, daily, Tel. 01993 811325. Built on the instructions of Queen Anne for the first Duke of Marlborough, who vanquished the French at the Battle of Blenheim in 1704, this palace, Ivory has noted, is the "quintessential stately pile of particular interest to Americans because of its Churchill (Jennie Jerome) and Vanderbilt associations," and "the sort of place of ultimate magnificence that a *real* Hollywood location scout would have tried to hire for Darlington Hall in *The Remains of the Day*."

Dorchester Abbey: off the A423, 6 miles southeast of Abingdon, open all year, daily, Tel. 01865 340007. The bridge across which Charles Wilcox drives the flustered Aunt Juley spans the Thames at Dorchester. The abbey church, founded circa 1140, contains a carving of sleeping monks being woken by a devil blowing a horn, and a fine effigy of the thirteenth-century crusader knight Sir John Holcombe, reaching expressively for his sword.

Mapledurham House: off the A4074, near Henley-on-Thames, open Easter Sunday to late September, certain days, Tel. 01734 723350. This red-brick Elizabethan mansion was visited in the eighteenth century by the crippled poet Alexander Pope, who dedicated several works to the ladies of the house, the beautiful sisters Martha and Teresa Blount. The Blounts, who were Roman Catholics, built a charming, pseudo-Gothic family chapel in the grounds. Observe the little window gable, high on the outside back wall, studded with oyster shells, a sign of safe refuge for Catholics.

Severn Valley Railway: Kidderminster station, west of Birmingham, in Hereford and Worcester, trains run from March to December, certain days, Tel. 01299 403816. The 16-mile trip on this standard-gauge steam railway runs from Kidderminster to Bridgnorth following the course of the River Severn and passing through the wooded heathland of the Wyre Forest. **Bewdley** station contains carriage and wagon workshops and a fine model railway.

Elgar's Birthplace: off the A44, 3 miles west of Worcester, open certain days, Tel. 01905 333224. Opposite this small Georgian house at Upper Broadheath are the Malvern Hills, from which Sir Edward Elgar (born 1857), composer of the *Enigma Variations*, sought solace and inspiration. There is a signposted "Elgar trail" for motorists.

Ludlow Castle: a few miles east of Brampton Bryan, across the Shropshire—Hereford border, open February to November, daily, Tel. 01584 873947. Ludlow Castle (the town name translates "the hill beside the loud water") was begun by the Norman knight Roger de Lacy to suppress the conquered Welsh. It rises from natural rock and few other castles in England can match its aura of impregnability. Napoleon's brother Lucien was held prisoner here in 1811.

In **London**, close to Victoria Square, which furnished the Schlegels' Wickham Place, is the **Queen's Gallery**, part of the Royal Mews, Buckingham Palace Road, SW1, open all year, certain days, Tel. 0171-799 2331. The gallery contains changing exhibitions from the immense royal collections: Prince Albert's photographs; paintings by Canaletto; Queen Alexandra's Fabergé eggs.

Tourist Information Centres/Accommodation: St. Aldate's, Oxford OX1 1DY; Tel. 01865 726871/ Fax 01865 252592. Town Hall, Market Place, Henley-on-Thames, Oxfordshire RG9 2AQ; Tel. 01491 578034. The Guildhall, High Street, Worcester WR1 2EY; Tel. 01905 726311/723471. **Travel London–Oxford**: Trains from Paddington station. By car, M25, M40, A40. **Oxford–Henley**: By car, A432, A4130. **London–Worcester**: Trains from Paddington station. By car, M25, M40, A34, A422.

The Remains of the Day

FATHER (*in his sepulchral voice*):
There was this English butler out in India—one day he goes to the dining room and what's he see under the table: a tiger. Not turning a hair, he goes to the drawing room—"Excuse me, m'lord"—(*gives imitation of polite cough*)—and whispering so as not to upset the ladies: "I'm very sorry, m'lord, there appears to be a tiger in the dining room. Perhaps his lordship will permit use of the twelve-bores?" They go on drinking their tea and then there's three gunshots. They don't think nothing of it—this being out in India where they're used to anything—and when the butler is back to refresh the teapots, he says, cool as a cucumber: "Dinner will be served at the usual time, m'lord, and I am pleased to say there will be no discernible traces left of the recent occurrence by that time."

—Shooting script (third draft), scene 22,
at the dinner table in the Servants' Hall

GRAND PIER

BADMINTON HOUSE: BAS-RELIEF WITH FOXES, A BACKDROP FOR EQUESTRIAN TROPHIES.

PAGES 96–97: THE GRAND PIER, WESTON-SUPER-MARE.

STEVENS THE BUTLER asks for a word with his employer, Lord Darlington. It concerns the housekeeper and the underbutler, who ran off together a month ago. He has found replacements: a Miss Kenton, a young woman, with excellent references and a very pleasing demeanour, and a man with considerable experience of butlering, but now of a certain age and happy to take on the post of underbutler. His Lordship, who is fingering a book, expresses no opinion: "Name?" "Stevens." Darlington raises an eyebrow. The old man, the prospective underbutler, turns out to be the butler's father, and is waiting outside the door. He is shown in. "Mr. Stevens. How do you do?" says Lord Darlington. Mr. Stevens, Sr., knowing better than to answer the question (he is arthritic and becoming forgetful), says simply, "M'lord." There is an exchange of pleasantries. Then the butler ushers out the new underbutler. At which point, during filming, a question arose: Should Lord Darlington (James Fox) shake hands with Mr. Stevens, Sr.? No one knew the etiquette of such a moment. Watching the scene, however, in his own library at Corsham Court, near Bath, was Lord Methuen. "Never," he said. "Never—never!"

The Remains of the Day (1993) is the story of an English butler's reconsideration of his life: before World War II, when he was master of Darlington Hall, Oxfordshire, when servants were hired on his say-so, and when he knew more clearly than his Lordship how many would be sitting down to dinner; and now, after the war, when the great house has been purchased by a retired American Congressman (Christopher Reeve), with a fondness for the English, but no real understanding of them, when the house lacks a housekeeper and is down to a skeleton staff, and when the future holds nothing for the butler but the prospect of emptiness and decay. Lord Darlington was an appeaser and a fascist fellow traveller, though no pantomime villain; perhaps, Stevens wonders, he was wrong to have reposed his faith in such a person, to have denied himself a life, either physical or emotional, in the service of a superior gentleman who was, in reality, no different from other men. Mr. Stevens fashioned a mask of perfect impassivity, became, by his own lights, a "well-contented man," justified himself to himself with a somewhat complacent self-satisfaction, but at the end of the day, he comes to recognize that shining silver, footmen with every button buttoned, and all the great feudal hierarchy of master and servants means nothing at all if compassion has been extinguished and the touch of a human hand denied.

The author of the novel, from which Ruth Jhabvala adapted Merchant Ivory's fourth English feature film, was Kazuo Ishiguro, who was born in Nagasaki in 1954, and who moved to England when he was six years old. Ishiguro has not turned his back on Japan quite so firmly as Ruth Jhabvala has turned

Badminton House: The servants' hall, adorned with superfluous trophies.

her back on Germany; but, like her, he writes only in English. He is a "foreigner" in Japan, in the sense that he barely speaks Japanese; and he considers himself English, in the sense that England is what he knows. He lives with his Scottish wife and their small daughter in Golders Green, north London, a few miles from the Hendon where Ruth Prawer spent her teenage years. Ishiguro's grandfather worked for Mr. Toyota, the founder of a Japanese automobile empire—but, Ishiguro remembers, Mr. Toyota drove a Rolls-Royce.

MISS KENTON (EMMA THOMPSON).

The world of Darlington Hall, on both sides of the baize door, is an imagined world. Ishiguro was educated by the state in the optimistic, liberal 1960s, not at a class-bound English private school; and he later attended the new universities of Kent and East Anglia, not the ancient institutions of Oxford or Cambridge. Lords and butlers belong to a world removed from his personal experience. "I'm very sloppy about names," Ishiguro said. "If I'm writing something, I hate having to stop and think up just the right name. If there's a book on the shelf in front of me, I usually get a name from that. There was a Blue Guide to England which I was using, published by Ernest Benn. So when I was looking for a name to give Miss Kenton when she gets married, I said, 'Ahh, Benn, that'll do.' I always promise myself, I'll tighten up these matters later on. But when I get to the end, the characters have been called by these names all along, and I can't be troubled to change them."

Had Ishiguro himself been present in Lord Methuen's private library, he would not have known, for certain, whether Lord Darlington would have allowed himself to shake hands with the distinguished underbutler (Peter Vaughan). Anthony Hopkins played Stevens the butler with faultless assurance. (Had Mr. Stevens, Jr., been the hero of his father's anecdote—had he been given the opportunity to demonstrate that "dignity" which distinguished the truly great butler—he would not, one may be sure, have hesitated one second before employing the twelve-bores on that impertinent Indian tiger.) But Anthony Hopkins did not know the correct form. He stipulated, Ivory noted, that an advisor should be on hand during shooting. "I don't know what butlers do," Hopkins had said.

Although he had directed many grand dinner parties, James Ivory himself was somewhat vague about the exact details of Lord Darlington's napery and glassware. Thus, Mr. Cyril Dickman, former senior steward in the royal household, was hired as the film's technical advisor. Mr. Dickman, however, was not present on that particular day at Corsham Court. "Cyril Dickman and his assistant Mr. Hamilton, who is still in service, came to us through Dame Guinevere Tilney," Ivory said. "Lady Tilney [a public servant who was at one time British representative to the U.N. Commission on the Status of Women] has opened several doors for Merchant Ivory that would otherwise have remained closed. She obtained permission, for example—and it took a great deal of doing—for us to shoot the Admiralty Arch scene in *Howards End*. Try to get in touch with that huge secret monolithic building at the beginning of The Mall and you get absolutely nowhere. There's no telephone. You can send a fax, but then nothing happens, no one replies. . . ."

The library at Powderham Castle: The repellent Mr. Spencer (Patrick Godfrey) attempts to demonstrate that the Common Man, here represented by Stevens the butler (Anthony Hopkins), has little knowledge of the great issues of the day—and hence is unfit to vote.

Corsham Court: Stevens (Anthony Hopkins) moves among the conference guests, cigarette box in hand.

Father (Peter Vaughan) on duty on the blue staircase, Powderham Castle.

⁂

JAMES IVORY read *The Remains of the Day* in 1989 in Kansas City during the production of *Mr. and Mrs. Bridge*, Ruth Jhabvala's adaptation of Evan Connell's two classic novels about the proprieties of middle-class, Midwestern life in the decade before World War II. "The actor in *Mr. and Mrs. Bridge* who played Grace Barron's husband—Remak Ramsay—gave me *The Remains of the Day*. It was a best-seller in America. He said, 'This'll be interesting to you'—but he let on that he'd dropped out halfway. He found it heavy going. But I loved it. I thought it would make a wonderful movie and was right up our alley." It turned out, however, that the playwright Harold Pinter, a friend of Ishiguro, had already optioned the book. Pinter had written a script, and the project was to be made by the anglophile American director Mike Nichols, and his partner John Calley, for Columbia Pictures.

Time passed. Nichols decided not to direct the film himself. An English director was hired. "The script was rewritten," Ivory said, "all unknown to Pinter, by the director [Chris Menaul], and then there were fireworks." The new director withdrew. And the project passed to M.I.P., Ivory having earlier let it be known at Columbia that *The Remains of the Day* was a film he would very much like to make. "We met Mike Nichols at the Russian Tea Room in New York," Ivory said. "Ruth was there. We all liked one another. The Pinter script was given to me. I read it, and I was sure that Ruth could improve on it. This was, after all, a Pinter script written for Mike Nichols; and what I wanted Ruth to write—and which she did write—was a James Ivory script for a Merchant Ivory film. That said, Ruth liked much of what Pinter had written, and her script incorporated many of his scenes."

Near the beginning of *The Remains of the Day*—the film that Ivory directed from the Jhabvala script—one of England's most prestigious clan gatherings of hounds and fox hunters, the Beaufort Hunt, assembles in front of Darlington Hall. The scene is a pure picture of Old England: ladies and gentlemen, clad in scarlet and navy blue, seated with assurance on handsome horses, greeting one another as old friends, confident of who they are and where they've come from. The staff pass among the horses with stirrup cups; Lord Darlington emerges from his house and, strolling among his guests, greets the Master of Foxhounds. Then, suddenly, amid the generalized bustle, the scene is given dramatic focus: Stevens, the invisible, ever-present servant, is observed impassively holding up a cup that an unseen rider never troubles to take. The hunt then rides away, majestically, and the scene ends.

Had much of Pinter's script survived in the film? "It has and it hasn't," Ishiguro said. "Ruth has often changed the words. But his contribution is there, although he may not want to think it is. Harold wished to use the hunt scene to reveal a latent nastiness and violence—the underbelly. On the surface, this grand ceremony; underneath, this boiling nastiness—which he's always interested in."

Catherine Freeman recalled her friend Ruth Jhabvala's attitude to England and English customs when they were both living in Delhi in the 1960s. "I cannot remember her speaking of England at all, the country or the place or anything to do with it, but she has always been intrigued by 'Englishness,' in a slightly ironic way. She would say, 'Ohh, so strong, so fine, so tall—how wonderful to be like you. . . .' She'd appear to admire all that, but with a sweet little edge of mockery, though mockery is too unkind a word."

THE WEST FRONT OF BADMINTON HOUSE, WITH A GLIMPSE OF ITS CONSERVATORIES, WHERE FATHER TRIPPED AND MISTER CHARLIE, THE HEAD FOOTMAN, STOLE A KISS. "PEOPLE USED TO LOOKING AT HOUSES—WHICH IS MOST PEOPLE—WILL BE PUZZLED AFTER SEEING *THE REMAINS OF THE DAY*," IVORY SAID. "THEY WILL CONCLUDE THAT FOR SOME ODD REASON DARLINGTON HALL HAD FIVE MAIN ELEVATIONS. THEY WILL BE RIGHT: TWO FROM BADMINTON AND THREE FROM DYRHAM PARK. PUT IT DOWN TO DIRECTORIAL EXCESS AND NOT TO THE CAPRICE OF ENGLISH LORDS."

LEFT: THE BEAUFORT HUNT ASSEMBLED IN THE RAIN AT DYRHAM PARK.

CORSHAM COURT: LORD DARLINGTON (JAMES FOX), AN ENGLISHMAN AT EASE.

The hunt was among the first scenes on the film's production schedule. It was set down for Dyrham Park, near Bath in the West Country, the late-seventeenth-century house, administered by the National Trust, which was to have furnished all the exterior shots of Darlington Hall. "When we came to shoot," Ivory said, "we found the house had been locked up, though they'd known for many days that we would be coming. They wouldn't put up the blinds and they wouldn't unlock the front door. We had long since negotiated that we could raise the blinds in the front of the house, so it wouldn't look as though no one lived there. It was beginning to rain. Outside was the Beaufort Hunt and the Duke of Beaufort, Anthony Hopkins, and James Fox; inside was a raging battle—we were demanding they open the doors.

"Look, it says in the script that Lord Darlington goes in and out of the door. But you never said you were going to use the interior of the house. (Unbelievable!) Yes, but it says in the script people pass in and out of the open doors. Have you not read the script? You've had it for at least a month. Then an official woman appeared. Are you telling me, I said, that you are going to keep Anthony Hopkins, James Fox, and the Beaufort Hunt out of this house? And then I said that I was going to the press, and we got into a tremendous row right there in the hall—and they opened the doors and pulled up the shades. Somewhat shamefacedly, the official woman admitted that she had not read the script. . . . Imagine! Lord Darlington wasn't to have been allowed to walk out of his own front door. Thirty years before, so to speak, that same door had been slammed in our faces. After that, we moved to Badminton House, owned by the Duke of Beaufort, with whom we had very pleasant dealings through the hunt—and he was pleased to have us."

⁂

WHEN THE Duke of Beaufort showed members of the production team round Badminton House, he unlocked one room which had been closed for many years. Inside was a cabinet filled with scores of glasses "I wish I'd known about these," he said. "I'm forever being sent out to buy new glasses." The room later became Miss Kenton's parlour. Another, smaller room was requisitioned for the spartan parlour, in which, resting briefly from his duties, Stevens sometimes allows himself a whisky and a small cigar. This room was the working centre of the butler's universe: here he devises his staff plan (an invention of Ishiguro). One day, Miss Kenton (Emma Thompson) brings a few flowers to brighten the room. Stevens is affronted by the intrusion. She is clever, assured, and a bit too pretty, and not afraid to answer back. No good can come of butlers and housekeepers and affairs of the heart. He retires into his shell, and does not miss an opportunity to pass comment on her work. She will not submit, however, to Mr. Stevens' persistent, niggling criticism. She points out his pigheadedness, which of course only makes him more pigheaded. And the more he criticizes her, the more she fights him, and the more tenderhearted she

STEVENS (ANTHONY HOPKINS) TRIES TO EXPLAIN THE FACTS OF LIFE TO LORD DARLINGTON'S NEPHEW, CARDINAL (HUGH GRANT), WHO IS SOON TO BE MARRIED.

Badminton House: Lord Darlington (James Fox, centre) assists the underbutler (Peter Vaughan), who, concentrating on his tea tray, has tripped on a paving stone.

Cardinal (Hugh Grant) in the music room at Powderham Castle.

Badminton House: On entering Darlington Hall—Stevens the butler (Anthony Hopkins), and a horse portrait by John Wootton.

Dyrham Park is—in James Ivory's judgment—one of England's most perfectly sited country houses. Here, as Darlington Hall, its contents are being auctioned after Lord Darlington's death in the 1950s.

Opposite: View from the George Inn at Norton St. Philip, near Bath. Stevens' borrowed Daimler can be seen heading past a timeless English parish church.

STEVENS (ANTHONY HOPKINS) ON HIS WEST COUNTRY TOUR WITH A LETTER FROM MISS KENTON.

grows—and the more frustrated. An affection between them, which, despite her efforts, never fully flowers, is the heart of this infinitely sad story.

The conjuring up of England—a specific prewar England, riven by real political conflicts, with real consequences; and a postwar England still haunted by the ghost of dead servicemen—has never been better achieved by Merchant Ivory. On Mr. Dickman's instructions, Stevens irons the newspaper page by page—and *The Times* in those days contained news, with a capital *N*, in the sense that Nirad Chaudhuri would have recognized it, not just a proliferation of airy, fluttering "sections." And later we see Stevens himself happily instructing a footman how to measure out the precise, immutable distance between table settings. The resulting banquet has exactly the right feel—when we come upon the end of it—of cracked walnuts and half-empty glasses of port. Lord Darlington sleeps in a camp bed, left over from the Great War, which he has set up at the end of his official bed, decorated with his earl's coronet. This larger bed is littered with his papers. This side of the film is handled with easy confidence. Ivory is familiar with the way Englishmen in evening dress are apt to behave, how they lounge in overstuffed armchairs, and how they treat their servants, both well and badly. All of which is a very long way from the eccentric Englishman with his wind-up gramophone in *The Householder*, and the abstracted cut-out couple, Sir Harry and Lady Cora, wandering lost among the revellers at the decadent house party in *Savages*.

Similarly, the backstairs life of this England—not the world of Leonard Bast, but of the flesh-and-blood people who keep the world of Darlington Hall going, who allow his Lordship the time to leaf through his books, to bone up at his leisure on the Jewish Question—is for the first time, in a sense, regarded straight on. As Mr. Stevens stands at the head of the dining table in the servants' hall and carves the intransigent roast pork, and the smallest maid hands round the brussels sprouts, there is the feeling of a scene there for its own sake and in its own right—the cross-hatching, as it were, which shadows the engraving—as much as for the workaday advancement of the plot.

THE PAVILION, WESTON-SUPER-MARE: MISS KENTON (NOW MRS. BENN) AND HER OLD FRIEND STEVENS MEET AFTER TWENTY YEARS. SHE LETS HIM DOWN GENTLY AS HE TRIES TO PERSUADE HER TO RETURN TO HER OLD POSITION AT DARLINGTON HALL.

⁂ ⁂ ⁂

IF MERCHANT IVORY'S ENGLAND is to be reduced to a single representative scene, it would not be Mrs. Wilcox and Margaret Schlegel in *Howards End*, two English friends, making a Christmas list while driving down The Mall; or Cecil, in *A Room with a View*, the English snob of snobs, seen in long shot in the garden at Windy Corner, all dignity gone, desperately swatting at a buzzing insect; or Maurice cocking a snook at English bigotry—and English sexual injustice—in the boathouse at Pendersleigh Park. It would, I think, be the scene in Mr. Stevens' parlour at Darlington Hall, when Miss Kenton—kind, spirited, beaten-down, but undefeated Miss Kenton—comes upon the butler in the half-light reading a book. The shooting script, scene 111, describes the scene thus:

MISS KENTON:
What are you reading?

STEVENS:
A book.

MISS KENTON:
Yes, but what sort of a book?

He looks up at her. She goes toward him. He shuts the book, stands, and holds it to his chest.

MISS KENTON:
What's your book? Are you shy about your book? Show it to me. Is it racy?

STEVENS:
Racy?

MISS KENTON:
Are you reading a racy book?

STEVENS:
You don't think "racy" books are to be found on his Lordship's shelves, do you?

MISS KENTON:
How would I know? What is it? Let me see it. Let me see your book.

STEVENS:
Miss Kenton, please leave me alone.

She smiles and moves closer to him. He wards her off.

MISS KENTON:
Why won't you show me your book?

STEVENS:
This is my private time. You are invading it.

MISS KENTON:
Oh, is that so? I am invading your private time, am I?

She moves closer.

MISS KENTON:
What's in that book? Come on. Let me see. Or are you protecting me? Is that what you are doing? Would I be shocked? Would it ruin my character?

They both stand quite still.

MISS KENTON:
Let me see it.

She gently begins to take the book from him, lifting his fingers one at a time from the book. This takes place in silence, their bodies very close. She opens the book and flicks through it.

MISS KENTON:
Oh dear, it's not scandalous at all. It's just a sentimental old love story.

They look at each other.

STEVENS:
I read these books—any books—to develop my command and knowledge of the English language. I read to further my education.

Pause.

STEVENS:
And now, Miss Kenton, I really must ask you not to disturb the very few moments of spare time I have to myself.

The scene is most beautifully played, with Miss Kenton gaining confidence, and playfulness, as she goes too far, edging Mr. Stevens into a corner, until he can retreat no further, and then peeling back his fingers only to find—that there is no mystery at all, that he is only reading, what?, a story by Miss Eleanor Lavish perhaps. Live England—the England of Lucy and her brother, Freddy Honeychurch, of Mr. Beebe and the Schlegel sisters, of Maurice and Alec Scudder—meets dead England, the England of Simcox, that other butler, of Dean Cornwallis with his face like a withered apple, of the noisy Blackshirt who throws his weight around at Lord Darlington's dinner table, and being, like Hitler, a vegetarian, demands to know precisely what has gone into the soup. . . . Time stands still in that moment, in the parlour, as the two irreconcilable Englands face up to each other in the twilight.

MISS KENTON (EMMA THOMPSON): "IT'S JUST A SENTIMENTAL OLD LOVE STORY."

Gazetteer

"Darlington Hall," Oxfordshire, was composed of three large West Country houses. **Dyrham Park**, near Bath, was in the first instance to have been used for all the exteriors of the hall. In the event, however, all that survives of Dyrham is the snaking opening shot, through the deer park to the front of the house; the gathering of the huntsmen (the Beaufort Hunt); the reverse-angle shot of Stevens looking through a window at Miss Kenton pedalling uphill on her bicycle; a night exterior; and the final aerial pull-away. **Saltram**, a few miles east of Plymouth, was an early candidate for the interiors of Darlington Hall. The house was Georgian with a medieval core; and Ivory was attracted, in particular, by its splendid saloon, designed by Robert Adam, and its kitchen, containing, among other items, six hundred copper utensils and a singular gas-heated food trolley.

The core of Darlington Hall, however, turned out, in the end, to be **Badminton House**, home of the Duke and Duchess of Beaufort, near Chipping Sodbury in Avon. The scenes in the great front hall, garden, conservatory, kitchen, and spacious servants' hall were all filmed there, as was the scene in the corridor, outside a Chinese bedroom, where Father falls sick. The ghostly shot of the footmen and the empty chairs at the beginning of the film was taken in the octagonal room at Badminton. Merchant Ivory copied the carpet in the Adam saloon at Saltram (at considerable cost), intending to lay it, for protection, over the original. However, when it became impossible for work to proceed at Saltram, the huge carpet was moved to **Powderham Castle**, near Exeter, home of the Courtenay family, the Earls of Devon. About half the interiors of Darlington Hall were photographed at Powderham: the famous blue staircase; the linked first and second libraries where the Baroness sings; and the music room where the banquet takes place, where Cardinal (Hugh Grant) is seen typing, and where the pigeon flutters in the dome.

The grand saloon at Saltram was replaced by the picture gallery at **Corsham Court**, the Wiltshire home of Lord Methuen. This gabled and pinnacled house, a former Elizabethan manor, had previously been used for a BBC TV adaptation of Jane Austen's *Northanger Abbey*. Merchant Ivory also filmed in the cabinet room at Corsham Court, which was used as a sitting room, the dining room, and in Lord Methuen's John Nash library. The panoramic view of the West Country, from the hillside where the Daimler runs out of fuel, was taken at sunset near the village of **Priddy**, on an outcrop of the **Chew Valley**, looking southwest toward Glastonbury, where it is said Joseph of Arimathea established the first Christian church in England, and where, as the "Isle of Avalon," King Arthur came to die.

The pub where Mr. Benn proposes to Miss Kenton was the **George Inn** at **Norton St. Philip**, reputedly the oldest licensed tavern in England (Judge Jeffreys stayed here while making his "hanging" western circuit, the Bloody Assizes); and that in which Stevens spends the night the **Hop Pole Inn**, at Limpley Stoke, both near Bath. The hotel at which Stevens pulls up (the **Royal Hotel**); the boardinghouse in which Miss Kenton is staying (the **Highbury Methodist Hotel**); the tearoom where she meets Mr. Stevens (the **Pavilion**); and the **Grand Pier** along which they stroll in the twilight were all at Weston-super-Mare, at the mouth of the River Severn, in Avon.

Dyrham Park: off the A46, 8 miles north of Bath, deer park open all year, afternoons daily, house and gardens open April to October, afternoons, certain days, Tel. 0117 937 2501. William Blathwayt, who married the heiress of

Powderham Castle. Once a fortified castle, with a moat and drawbridge, it has been associated with the Courtenay family, Earls of Devon, for nearly six hundred years. In appearance it is exactly the kind of storybook castle that James Ivory describes in the foreword to this book and could have been the model for the one his father fashioned for him out of Oregon pine.

Dyrham in 1689, employed the architect William Talman to rebuild the baroque east front (seen in the film). Before becoming Secretary of State to William III, Blathwayt worked in the Plantations Office in Whitehall and was much involved with the administration of the young American colonies.

Badminton House: off the B4040, east of Chipping Sodbury. The immense ancestral home of the Beauforts began as a late-Tudor house, but was substantially rebuilt in the 1740s. The third Duke brought many paintings and marbles from Rome, and commissioned Wootton to paint the huge canvases for the remodelled entrance hall (where the game of badminton was invented in 1836). Closed to the public, but groups wishing to visit should apply to Her Grace the Duchess of Beaufort, Badminton House, Badminton, Avon GL9 1DB.

Powderham Castle: off the A379, 8 miles southeast of Exeter, Devon, open April to October, certain days, Tel. 01626 890243. The medieval castle, built by Sir Philip Courtenay, between 1390 and 1420, was severely damaged during the Civil War and restored as a manor house in the eighteenth century. The house contains many rococo ceilings and marble fireplaces, and much fine Stuart and Regency furniture, but its outstanding features are the staircase hall, with ornate plasterwork against a brilliant blue-green background, and the music room, with its baroque organ, scene of the film's great banquet.

"Powderham Castle," Ivory adds, "was where the immensely rich William Beckford, builder of the legendary treasure house, Fonthill Abbey, came to grief in a famous sexual scandal of 1784, when, there on a visit aged twenty-four, he was caught with the sixteen-year-old 'Kitty' (William) Courtenay by a Simcox-like family retainer who heard 'a creeking and bustle, which raised his curiosity, & thro' the key hole he saw the operation, which it seems he did not interrupt, but informed Lord C, & the whole was blown up.'

"Beckford explained to the latter that he had been merely thrashing his son, but Kitty was forced to give up incriminating letters. Far too rich to be put to death, Beckford had to flee for a time to Portugal. Whether the pair were caught in the room with the gilded bed surmounted by an earl's coronet, at the foot of which Lord Darlington slept, is not told to the public, and the M.I.P. crew felt it was indiscreet to ask. Kitty Courtenay survived the scandal, and for his twenty-first birthday party had the splendid music room built by Wyatt in which, as noted above, we mounted the appeaser's banquet."

Corsham Court: Corsham, Wiltshire, on the A4 between Chippenham and Bath, open January to November, certain days, Tel. 01249 712214. The chief attraction of Corsham, the grounds of which were laid out by Capability Brown, is its collection of statuary, bronzes, and more than 140 paintings by, among others, Caravaggio, Reynolds, Rubens, Van Dyck, and Fra Filippo Lippi.

Ham Hill Country Park: off the A3088, 8 miles west of Yeovil, Somerset, open all year, daily, Tel. 01935 75272/823617. There are panoramic views of Somerset from the Iron Age mounds at the crest of this 426-foot hill.

Dyrham Park, Badminton, and especially Corsham Court are very near **Bath**, England's most famous and most ancient spa, renowned in the eighteenth century as a centre of social style and architectural elegance (**Queen's Square**, the **Assembly Rooms**, and the incomparable **Royal Crescent**). "A splendid place to stay," Ivory commented, "to eat in, and to poke about in, even if one's *not* especially interested in eighteenth-century architecture and city planning."

Tourist Information Centres/Accommodation: The Guildhall, High Street, Bath, Avon BA1 1SW; Tel. 01225 462831. Civic Centre, Paris Street, Exeter, Devon EX1 1JJ; Tel. 01392 265700/Fax 01392 265265. Beach Lawns, Weston-super-Mare, Avon BS23 1AT; Tel. 01934 626838. **Travel London–Bath**: Trains from Paddington station. By car, M25, M4, A46, A4. **London–Exeter**: Trains from Paddington station. By car, M25, M3, A30, A34, A303.

Filmography

In the following credit lists "[thus]" is used to indicate the correct spelling of certain on-screen names.

A Room with a View
U.K. 35mm. colour (Fuji). Screen ratio 1:1.66. Dolby Stereo. 10,501 feet, 117 minutes.

Production company: Merchant Ivory Productions [London] for Goldcrest Films & Television with the National Film Finance Corporation, Curzon Film Distributors, and Film Four International [all London]. © A Room with a View Productions, Ltd., 1985. *First release:* (U.S.) Paris Theater, New York, March 7, 1986; (U.K.) Curzon [Mayfair], London, April 11, 1986.

Producer: Ismail Merchant. *Associate producers:* Paul Bradley; (Italy) Peter Marangoni. *Production managers:* Ann Wingate, Lanfranco Diotallevi. *Production coordinator:* Caroline Hill. *Location manager:* (England) Jilly Gutteridge. *Production secretaries:* Lisa Strout, Nicky Kentish Barnes. *Production assistants:* Andrew Bergen, Daniele Nepi, Nayeem Hafizka, Paul Scacchi, Carlo Mantegazza, Elizabeth Swisher, Jane Delandro. *Production accountants:* Alan John, Sunil Kirparam, Luigi Riitano.

Director: James Ivory. *Assistant director:* Kevan Barker. *Second assistant directors:* Daniel Sonnis, Simon Moseley. *Casting:* Celestia Fox. *Continuity:* Renée Glynne. *Assistants to the director:* Pippo Pisciotto, (special) Linsey Lee.

Screenplay: Ruth Prawer Jhabvala, based on the novel by E. M. Forster.

Photography: Tony Pierce-Roberts. *Follow focus:* Graham Hazard. *Clapper-loader:* Jonathan Earp. *Camera assistants:* Phillip Sindall, Steve Dembitzer. *Second unit camera:* Sergio Melaranci, (assistant) Adriano Gangi. *Processed and printed by:* Technicolor, London. *Grips:* Malcolm Huse, Sergio Serantoni, Angelo Tiberti. *Gaffers:* Luigi Bisioli, Lou Bogue. *Best boys:* Glen Parsons, Alvaro Romagnoli. *Electricians:* Harry Bisson, Aldo Laureti, Marco Romagnoli, Steve Senior. *Stills:* Sarah Quill, Katya Grenfell.

Music: Richard Robbins. *Music orchestrated and conducted by:* Francis Shaw, Barrie Guard. *Music producer:* Simon Heyworth. *Music extracts:* "O mio babbino caro" from *Gianni Schicchi*, "Chi il bel sogno di Doretta" [thus] from *La Rondine*, by Giacomo Puccini, performed by Kiri Te Kanawa and the London Philharmonic Orchestra, conducted by Sir John Pritchard; "Mademoiselle Modiste," by Victor Herbert, performed by The Dryden Orchestra of the Eastman School of Music.

Editor: Humphrey Dixon. *Assistant editors:* Paul Keye, Jr., Joanna Jimenez, Kevin Brooks.

Production design: Gianni Quaranta, Brian Ackland-Snow. *Art directors:* Brian Savegar, Elio Altamura. *Title design:* Chris Allies. *Title backgrounds:* Folco Cianfanelli. *Assistant art directors:* Stefano Secchi, Anita Overland, Roberto Galante, Malachi Smyth. *Set dressers:* Floriano Porzionato, Dennis Simmonds, Mick Flanders. *Construction managers:* Bob Cross, Franco Pizzonia.

Costume design: Jenny Beavan, John Bright. *Costume coordinator:* William Peirce [thus]. *Assistant costume designer:* Sally Turner. *Costume supervisors:* Brenda Dabbs, (assistant) Elena Puliti. *Costumes:* Cosprop, London. *Makeup:* Christine Beveridge, (assistant) Sally Harrison. *Hairdresser:* Carol Hemming, (assistant) Paolo Mantini.

Riggers: Massimo Fantauzzi, Dennis Harrison. *Property masters:* Dennis Fruin, Goffredo Massetti. *Standby props:* Mark Fruin, Kieron McNamara [thus]. *Props buyer:* Jeanne Vertigan. *Carpenters:* Bob Coleman, Roy Hansford, Ulderico Nanni. *Painters:* John Chapple, James Ede, Antonio Vandilli, Umberto Vandilli. *Stagehands:* James Loftus, Len Serpant. *Transport:* Carlo Quinterio. *Publicity:* Zakiya Powell.

Sound: Ray Beckett. *Boom operator:* Nick Hammond. *Sound editors:* Tony Lenny, Peter Compton, Alan Killick. *Assistant sound editors:* Anna Shepherd, Phillip Alton, Tom Freeman. *Italian revoicing:* Dino Colizzi. *Music recording:* Brian Masterson (Windmill Lane Studios, Dublin). *Sound rerecording:* Richard King (World Wide Sound, London).

Cast: (in Florence) Maggie Smith (*Charlotte Bartlett, a chaperon*), Helena Bonham Carter (*Lucy Honeychurch, Miss Bartlett's cousin and charge*), Denholm Elliott (*Mr. Emerson, an English tourist*), Julian Sands (*George Emerson*), Simon Callow (*the Reverend Mr. Beebe*), Patrick Godfrey (*the Reverend Mr. Eager, Chaplain of the Anglican Church in Florence*), Judi Dench (*Eleanor Lavish, a novelist*), Fabia Drake and Joan Henley (*The Misses Catharine and Teresa Alan*), Amanda Walker (*the Cockney Signora*); (in England) Daniel Day Lewis (*Cecil Vyse*), Maria Britneva (*Mrs. Vyse, Cecil's mother*), Rosemary Leach (*Mrs. Honeychurch*), Rupert Graves (*Freddy Honeychurch*), Peter Cellier (*Sir Harry Otway, a landlord*), Mia Fothergill (*Minnie Beebe*); (and) Kitty Aldridge (*New Lucy*), Brigid Erin Bates (*Maid at Windy Corner*), Isabella Celani (*Persephone*), Luigi Di Fiori (*Murdered Youth*), Matyelock Gibbs (*New Charlotte*), Mirio Guidelli (*Santa Croce Guide*), Freddy Korner (*Mr. Floyd*), Patty Lawrence (*Mrs. Butterworth*), Elizabeth Marangoni (*Miss Pole*), Peter Munt (*Coachman*), Lucca Rossi (*Phaeton*), Stefano Serboli (*Fighting Youth*), Phillada Sewell and Margaret Ward (*Ladies at Sir Harry's Garden Party*).

Maurice

U.K./U.S.A. 35mm. colour (Fuji). Screen ratio 1:1.66. Dolby Stereo. 12,607 feet, 140 minutes.

Production company: Merchant Ivory Productions [London] with Cinecom Pictures [New York City] and Film Four International [London]. © Maurice Productions, Ltd., 1987. *Premiere:* Venice Film Festival, August 29, 1987. *First release:* (U.S.) Paris Theater, New York, September 18, 1987; (U.K.) Cannon cinemas, Shaftesbury Avenue and Fulham Road, London, November 6, 1987.

Producer: Ismail Merchant. *Associate producer:* Paul Bradley. *Production supervisor:* Raymond Day. *Production coordinator:* Joyce Turner. *Location managers:* Maggie Parsons, Natasha Grenfell. *Location scout:* Joe Friedman. *Production assistants:* Nicky Kentish Barnes, Ben Barker. *Production accountants:* William Tyler, Sunil Kirparam. *Producer's secretary:* Arbell Lowther.

Director: James Ivory. *First assistant directors:* Michael Zimbrich, Kevan Barker. *Second assistant directors:* Lee Cleary, John Phelan. *Third assistant director:* Simon Moseley. *Casting:* Celestia Fox. *Continuity:* Lorely Farley.

Screenplay: Kit Hesketh-Harvey, James Ivory, from the novel by E. M. Forster.

Photography: Pierre Lhomme. *Camera operators:* Nigel Willoughby, Tony Woodcock. *Camera focus:* Tim Dodd [thus]. *Clapper-loader:* Gerry Altman. *Processed and printed by:* Technicolor, London. *Gaffer:* Jack Collins. *Grip:* Kevin Fraser. *Best boy:* Steve Costello. *Stills:* Jon Gardey [thus], Katya Grenfell.

Music: Richard Robbins. *Conductor:* Harry Rabinowitz. *Music extract:* Miserere, Psalm 51, by Gregorio Allegri, sung by the Choir of King's College, Cambridge. *Music associate:* Bob Stewart.

Editor: Katherine Wenning. *Assistant editor:* Andrew Marcus. *Apprentice picture editor:* Stacia Thompson. *Opticals:* Peerless Camera Company, Ltd., London.

Production design: Brian Ackland-Snow. *Art directors:* Peter James, Brian Savegar. *Title design:* Chris Allies. *Assistant set dresser:* Amanda Ackland-Snow.

Costume design: Jenny Beavan, John Bright. *Co-costume designer:* William Peirce [thus]. *Wardrobe master:* Raymond Usher Cooper. *Wardrobe assistant:* Jane Burton. *Makeup:* Mary Hillman. *Hairdresser:* Carol Hemming, (assistant) Paolo Mantini.

Stunts: Harvey Kip, Adrian Ffooks. *Property master:* Dennis Fruin. *Standby props:* Bill Coggan, Rob Hill. *Unit publicist:* Mira Stout.

Sound: Mike Shoring. *Boom operator:* Andy Morris. *Sound editor:* Tony Lenny. *Dialogue editor:* Alan Killick. *Footsteps editor:* Howard Lanning. *Assistant sound editors:* Max Hoskins, Anna Shepherd, Tom Freeman. *Music recording:* Brian Masterson (Windmill Lane Studios, Dublin). *Music editor:* Mark Potter, Jr. *Sound rerecording:* Richard King (World Wide Sound, London).

Cast: James Wilby (*Maurice Hall*), Hugh Grant (*Clive Durham*), Rupert Graves (*Alec Scudder*), Denholm Elliott (*Dr. Barry*), Simon Callow (*Mr. Ducie*), Billie Whitelaw (*Mrs. Hall*), Ben Kingsley (*Lasker Jones*), Judy Parfitt (*Mrs. Durham*), Phoebe Nicholls (*Anne Woods, Mrs. Clive Durham*), Mark Tandy (*Viscount Risley*), Helena Michell (*Ada Hall*), Kitty Aldridge (*Kitty Hall*), Patrick Godfrey (*Simcox*), Michael Jenn (*Archie*), Barry Foster (*Dean Cornwallis*), Peter Eyre (*the Reverend Mr. Borenius*), Catherine Rabett (*Pippa Durham*), Orlando Wells (*Young Maurice*), Helena Bonham Carter (*Lady at Cricket Match*), Mark Payton (*Chapman*), Maria Britneva (*Mrs. Sheepshanks*), John Elmes (*Hill*), Alan Foss (*Old Man on Train*), Philip Fox (*Dr. Jowitt*), Olwen Griffiths (*Mrs. Scudder*), Chris Hunter (*Fred Scudder*), Gerard McArthur (*Third Undergraduate*), Breffni McKenna (*Guardsman*), Miles Richardson (*First Undergraduate*), Phillada Sewell (*Matron*), Matthew Sim (*Fetherstonhaugh*), Andrew St. Clair (*Second Undergraduate*), Harriet Thorpe (*Barmaid*), Julian Wadham (*Hull*), Richard Warner (*Judge*), Alan Whybrow (*Mr. Scudder*).

Howards End

U.K./U.S.A./Japan. Super-35 colour (Eastman Kodak). Screen ratio 1:2.35. Dolby Stereo. 12,802 feet, 142 minutes.

Production company: Merchant Ivory Productions [London/New York] with Sumitomo Corporation, Imagica Corporation, Cinema Ten Corporation, JSB Japan Satellite Broadcasting, Inc., Ide Productions [all Tokyo], and Film Four International [London]. © Merchant Ivory Productions, Ltd., 1991. *First release:* (U.S.) Paris Theater, New York, March 13, 1992; (U.K.) Curzon Mayfair, London, May 1, 1992.

Producer: Ismail Merchant. *Coproducer:* Ann Wingate. *Executive producer:* Paul Bradley. *Associate producer:* Donald Rosenfeld. *Production managers:* John Downes, Caroline Hill. *Production coordinator:* Nick O'Hagan. *Location scout:* Joe Friedman. *Location manager:* Jeanne Ferber. *Location assistant:* Christian McWilliams. *Production accountants:* Mike Yell, Sunil Kirparam. *Assistant accountant:* Frances Richardson. *Assistant to the producer:* Kathryn Martin. *Production runner:* Jo Chate. *Production assistants:* James Butler, Flora Herbert, Benjamin Howarth, Fay Efrosini Lellios, Don Rogers, Emily Shapland.

Director: James Ivory. *Assistant director:* Chris Newman. *Second assistant director:* Simon Moseley. *Third assistant director:* Carl Oprey. *Casting:* Celestia Fox. *Continuity:* Jean Bourne.

Screenplay: Ruth Prawer Jhabvala, based upon the novel by E. M. Forster.

Photography: Tony Pierce-Roberts. *Follow focus cameraman:* Rawdon Hayne. *Clapper-loader:* Peter Batten. *Camera trainee:* Roderick Marley. *Processed and printed by:* Technicolor, London. *Grip:* Malcolm Huse. *Gaffer:* Tommy Finch. *Best boy:* Billy Pochetty. *Stills:* Derrick Santini.

Music: Richard Robbins. *Conductor:* Harry Rabinowitz. *Music performed by:* The English Chamber Orchestra. *Piano soloist:* Martin Jones. *Tangos performed by:* Teddy Peiro and his Tango Group. *Music extracts:* "Bridal Lullaby," "Mock Morris," by Percy Grainger. *Music associate:* Robert Stewart. *Music coordinator:* Geoff Alexander.

Editor: Andrew Marcus. *Associate editors:* Michelle Gorchow, James Marsh. *Assistant editors:* Tom Freeman, (second) Paul Dawson. *Optical effects:* Peerless Camera Company, Ltd., London; Optical Film Effects, Ltd.

Production design: Luciana Arrighi. *Art director:* John Ralph. *Set decorator:* Ian Whittaker. *Title design:* Oliver Harrison. *Art department assistant:* Philip Robinson. *Construction manager:* John Hedges.

Costume design: Jenny Beavan, John Bright. *Wardrobe supervisors:* Stephen Cornish, Sue Honeybourne. *Wardrobe assistants:* Jill Avery, Adrian Simmonds. *Costumes:* Cosprop, London. *Chief makeup:* Christine Beveridge. *Makeup assistant:* Sally Jaye. *Chief hairdresser:* Carol Hemming. *Assistant hairdresser:* Paolo Mantini. *Hair/makeup trainee:* Sian Grigg.

Production buyer: Jill Quertier. *Property master:* Barry Wilkinson. *Dressing props:* Charlie Ixer, Peter Wallis. *Standby props:* Simon Wilkinson, Gary Ixer. *Chargehand carpenter:* Michael Hedges. *Chargehand painter:* Robin Heinson. *Standbys:* Richard Jones, Jeff Sullivan, Bill Richards, Len Serpant. *Transport captain:* Michael Lind. *Special effects:* Effects Associates.

Sound recordist: Mike Shoring. *Boom operator:* Andy Morris. *Supervising sound editor:* Campbell Askew. *Dialogue editor:* Sarah Morton. *Assistant sound editor:* Bettina McCall. *Music recording:* Keith Grant. *Rerecording mixers:* Robin O'Donoghue, Dominic Lester (Twickenham Film Studios, Middlesex).

Cast in order of appearance: Vanessa Redgrave (*Ruth Wilcox*), Helena Bonham Carter (*Helen Schlegel*), Joseph Bennett (*Paul Wilcox*), Emma Thompson (*Margaret Schlegel*), Prunella Scales (*Aunt Juley*), Adrian Ross Magenty (*Tibby Schlegel*), Jo Kendall (*Annie*), Anthony Hopkins (*Henry Wilcox*), James Wilby (*Charles Wilcox*), Jemma Redgrave (*Evie Wilcox*), Ian Latimer (*Station Master*), Samuel West (*Leonard Bast*), [Simon Callow (*Speaker on "Music and Meaning"*).] Mary Nash (*Pianist*), Siegbert Prawer (*Man Asking a Question*), Susie Lindeman (*Dolly Wilcox*), Nicola Duffett (*Jacky Bast*), Mark Tandy, Andrew St. Clair, Anne Lambton, Emma Godfrey, Duncan Brown, Iain Kelly (*Luncheon Guests*), Atlanta White (*Maid at Howards End*), Gerald Paris (*Porphyrion Supervisor*), Allie Byrne, Sally Geoghegan, Paula Stockbridge, Bridget Duvall, Lucy Freeman, Harriet Stewart, Tina Leslie (*Blue-stockings*), Mark Payton (*Percy Cahill*), David Delaney (*Simpson's Carver*), Mary McWilliams (*Wilcox Baby*), Barbara Hicks (*Miss Avery*), Rodney Rymell (*Chauffeur*), Luke Parry (*Tom, the farmer's boy*), Antony Gilding (*Bank Supervisor*), Peter Cellier (*Colonel Fussell*), Crispin Bonham Carter (*Albert Fussell*), Patricia Lawrence, Margery Mason (*Wedding Guests*), Jim Bowden (*Martlett*), Alan James (*Porphyrion Chief Clerk*), Jocelyn Cobb (*Telegraph Operator*), Peter Darling (*Doctor*), Terence Sach (*Delivery Man*), Brian Lipson (*Police Inspector*), Barr Heckstall-Smith (*Helen's Child*).

THE REMAINS OF THE DAY

U.S.A./U.K. Super-35 colour (Eastman Kodak). Screen ratio 1:2.35. Dolby Stereo. 12,069 feet, 134 minutes.

Production company: Merchant Ivory Productions [London/New York] with Mike Nichols and John Calley [New York City] for Columbia Pictures [Los Angeles]. © Columbia Pictures, Inc., 1993. *Premiere:* The Academy of Motion Picture Arts and Sciences, Los Angeles, October 25, 1993. *First release:* (U.S.) Paris Theater, New York, November 5, 1993; (U.K.) Curzon Mayfair, London, November 12, 1993.

Producers: Ismail Merchant; Mike Nichols, John Calley. *Executive producer:* Paul Bradley. *Associate producer:* Donald Rosenfeld. *Production supervisor:* Joyce Herlihy. *Production coordinator:* Lorraine Fennell. *Location scout:* Joe Friedman. *Location manager:* Christian McWilliams. *Location assistant:* Colin Plenty. *Production accountants:* Bob Blues, Sunil Kirparam, Jacky Holding. *Assistant to the producer:* Kathryn Martin. *Project creative assistant:* Fay Efrosini Lellios.

Director: James Ivory. *First assistant director:* Chris Newman. *Second assistant director:* Simon Moseley. *Third assistant director:* Bernard Bellew. *Director's runner:* Peter Giblin. *Casting:* Celestia Fox. *Script supervisor:* Diana Dill.

Screenplay: Ruth Prawer Jhabvala, based on the novel by Kazuo Ishiguro.

Photography: Tony Pierce-Roberts. *Follow focus cameraman:* Rawdon Hayne. *Clapper-loader:* Peter Batten. *Second unit cameraman:* Roger Pearce. *Camera trainee:* Roderick Marley. *Camera apprentice:* Damienne Caron. *Camera grip:* Malcolm Huse. *Processed and printed by:* Technicolor, London. *Gaffer:* Tommy Finch. *Best boy:* Les Weighell. *Stills photographer:* Derrick Santini.

Music: Richard Robbins. *Orchestral arrangements:* Robert Stewart. *Conductor:* Harry Rabinowitz. *Songs:* "Blue Moon," by Richard Rodgers, Lorenz Hart; "Roll Along Prairie Moon," by Ted Fiorito, Albert Von Tilzer, Harry MacPherson, sung by Gracie Fields; "Sei Mir Gegrüsst," by Franz Schubert, sung by Ann Murray, piano Graham Johnson. *Music coordinator:* Geoff Alexander. *Choreographer:* Elizabeth Aldrich.

Editor: Andrew Marcus. *Associate editor:* Michelle Gorchow. *Assistant editor:* Kerry Kohler. *Second assistant editor:* Simon Cozens. *Apprentice editor:* Craig Mooney. *Titles and opticals:* Peerless Camera Company, Ltd., London.

Production design: Luciana Arrighi. *Art director:* John Ralph. *Set decorator:* Ian Whittaker. *Construction manager:* John Hedges. *Art department assistants:* Sophia Mueller, Sveva Costa Sanservino, Simone Assanand.

Costume design: Jenny Beavan, John Bright. *Wardrobe mistress:* Sue Honeybourne. *Wardrobe assistants:* Adrian Simmonds, Jill Avery, Victoria Harwood. *Costumes:* Cosprop, London. *Chief makeup artist:* Christine Beveridge. *Makeup artist:* Norma Webb. *Chief hairdresser:* Carol Hemming. *Hairdresser:* Paolo Mantini.

Production buyer: Jill Quertier. *Property master:* Arthur Wicks. *Standby props:* Mark Fruin, Chris Browning. *Dressing props:* Dennis Simmonds. *Crowd marshal:* William James. *Technical advisor:* Cyril Dickman, M.V.O., R.V.M. *Assistant advisor:* Robert Hamilton, R.V.M. *Stand-ins:* Annie Livings, David Field. *Unit drivers:* Cengiz Asiliskender, Bryan Baverstock, David Bennett, John Bower.

Sound recordist: David Stephenson. *Boom operator:* Colin Wood. *Sound rerecording:* Robin O'Donoghue, (assistant) Dominic Lester (Twickenham Film Studios, Middlesex). *On-set sound assistant:* Aaron Anawalt. *Sound editor:* Colin Miller. *Dialogue editor:* Derek Holding. *Foley editor:* Brian Blamey. *Assistant sound editors:* Russ Woolnough, Geoff R. Brown. *Music recording engineer:* Bill Sommerville-Large (Windmill Lane Studios, Dublin).

Cast in order of appearance: John Haycraft (*Auctioneer*), Christopher Reeve (*Lewis*), Anthony Hopkins (*Stevens*), Emma Thompson (*Miss Kenton*), Caroline Hunt (*Landlady*), James Fox (*Lord Darlington*), Peter Vaughan (*Father*), Paula Jacobs (*Mrs. Mortimer, the cook*), Ben Chaplin (*Charlie, head footman*), Steve Dibben (*George, second footman*), Abigail Harrison (*Housemaid*), Patrick Godfrey (*Spencer*), Peter Cellier (*Sir Leonard Bax*), Peter Halliday (*Canon Tufnell*), Hugh Grant (*Cardinal*), Terence Bayler (*Trimmer*), Jeffry Wickham (*Viscount Bigge*), Hugh Sweetman (*Scullery Boy*), Michael Lonsdale (*Dupont D'Ivry*), Brigitte Kahn (*Baroness*), John Savident (*Dr. Meredith*), Tony Aitken (*Postmaster*), Emma Lewis (*Elsa*), Joanna Joseph (*Irma*), Rupert Vansittart (*Sir Geoffrey Wren*), Tim Pigott-Smith (*Benn*), Christopher Brown (*Wren's Friend*), Lena Headey (*Lizzie*), Paul Copley (*Harry Smith*), Ian Redford (*Publican*), Jo Kendall (*Publican's Wife*), Steven Beard (*Andrews*), Pip Torrens (*Dr. Carlisle*), Frank Shelley (*Prime Minister*), Peter Eyre (*Lord Halifax*), Jestyn Phillips (*Foreign Office Official*), Wolf Kahler (*German Ambassador*), Frank Höltje, Andreas Töns (*German Foreign Office Officials*), Roger McKern (*Police Constable*), Angela Newmarch (*Waitress*).

Index

Italic page numbers refer to illustrations and captions.

Photograph Credits

Most of the photographs of films used in this book are © Merchant Ivory Productions (M.I.P.). However, photographs from *The Remains of the Day* (pp. 8, 13, 96–97, 98, 100–104, 106–14, 117, 119) are © M.I.P./Columbia Pictures, Inc., 1993. Below are additional photographers' credits, listed alphabetically and followed by page number:

British Film Institute (Stills, Posters and Designs): 21 (both); Christopher Cormack: 31 (both); Kathleen Culbert-Aguilar: 10–11; Jon Gardey: 1, 2–3, 12, 14–15, 52–53, 54, 56–63, 65 (right), 67 (below), 68–71; Katya Grenfell: 64–65, 66–67, 67 (top); Mary Ellen Mark: 28 (right); Subrata Mitra: 25, 26; T. S. Nagarajan: 27 (left); The Photo Studios, New Delhi: 17; Popperfoto, London: 89; Sarah Quill: 32–33, 34, 36, 37, 38 (both), 39, 40–49; Juan Quirno: 29, 30; Morgan Renard: 19; Derrick Santini: 8, 13, 74–75, 76, 78–92, 96–97, 98, 100–104, 106–14, 117, 119.

The map of "Merchant Ivory's English Locations" appearing on page 7 was created by Hal Just.